The Egyptian Red Sea
A Diver's Guide

Two coral pillars, rising from 50 feet, form the center of The Temple, one of Sinai's most picturesque dive sites.

The Egyptian Red Sea
A Diver's Guide

by Eric Hanauer

Watersport Publishing, Inc.
San Diego, California

First Printing 1988
Watersport Publishing, Inc., P.O. Box 83727, San Diego, CA 92138

Printed in Singapore through Palace Press.

ISBN 0-922769-04-4

Library of Congress Catalog Card Number: 88-51679
Hanauer, Eric
        The Egyptian Red Sea: A Diver's Guide

Table of Contents

Acknowledgements

Attempting to write a Red Sea diver's guide without a lot of help would have been impossible. This writer was fortunate to receive an abundance, through four challenging years since the inception of this project. I would like to express my appreciation to everyone by crediting their contributions here.

The idea originated with Hani El Meniawi of Diving and International Ventures, a pioneer Egyptian diving instructor and tour operator. It was focused more sharply by Richard Stewart of Sport Diver Publications. Both of them provided expertise, encouragement, and logistical support on the early trips.

My wife, Mia Tegner, filled many roles in the production of this book. Her knowledge of marine biology was invaluable, as was her beautiful work as an underwater model. She wrote the chapter on the science of the Red Sea, and served as the critical editor that every author needs. She calmed me down when things got exciting, and picked me up when they went wrong.

Rolf Schmidt and Abdel Moneim Rashad initiated the support to launch the book, and stuck with us through many setbacks. Rolf, manager of Sinai Divers, provided invaluable insights on marine life and dive areas, gained in 15 years of running Red Sea dive operations. Moneim, US west coast director of the Egyptian Tourist Authority, spearheaded his agency's support of this book, and also helped edit the chapters on topside Egypt.

Dive guides, both in Sinai and Hurghada, were generous in sharing their experience and hard-earned knowledge about the dive sites. Without their help, this book could not have been written. They are: Hisham Gabr Aly, Ali Saad El Din, Terry Kennedy, Ayman Kamel, Mohamed Kabany, Rudi Kneip, Jeremy McWilliam, Hani El Meniawi, Rolf Schmidt, and Dr. Adel Taher. Additional information came from Georg Flashar, Dr. Amatzia Genin, Bob Johnson, Dr. Hani Khalil, Captain George Lechler, and Mohammed Shaffei. Valued friends and diving buddies in the Red Sea also included Jodi Butler, Mike Curtis, Frauke Hargesheimer, Anita Hess, Beth Stewart, and Klaus Zwenig.

Mohammed Nassim, Salah El Derwi, Dr. Shawki Hussein, and Ossama Nassar of the Egyptian Tourist Authority provided encouragement and logistical support.

Ken Loyst of Watersport Publishing had the vision and the fortitude to adopt this project and see it through to completion. Every time hard decisions had to be made, he chose the quality solution over economical expediency.

While her father was having fun underwater, Sandi Hanauer took care of things on the home front.

Bonnie Cardone, executive editor of Skin Diver Magazine, gave this fledgling author his first opportunity 11 years ago, and helped him learn the craft on the job.

The following companies provided support: DIVE, Egypt Air, Ikelite, Oceanic, Scubapro, Seapro, Sinai Divers, Sinai Hotels and Diving Clubs.

To the memory of Admiral H. N. Hallouda, and Herb and Cora Taylor.

To everyone mentioned here, and to anyone I might have inadvertently forgotten, my heartfelt thanks.

Eric Hanauer
Costa Mesa, California
September, 1988

PREFACE

When the northern Red Sea was consolidated under Egyptian control, it became obvious that there was a need for a new divers' guidebook to the area. The only one previously available was Shlomo Cohen's *Red Sea Diver's Guide*, first published in Israel in 1975. A beautifully illustrated book in full color, it was intended as a do-it-yourself beach diving guide for the eastern coast of Sinai. Its aerial photographs and translucent overlays enabled divers to find the dive sites by driving over dirt roads and entering from the beaches. Unfortunately, security considerations at the time prohibited the inclusion of some of the best diving spots in the Sharm El Sheikh area.

Cohen's book is still the best source available for the northern Sinai region, including Eilat and Nuweiba. However, the amount of coastline accessible to divers has increased nearly tenfold. And most sites can no longer be dived by an individual on his or her own; the services of a guide are needed.

These circumstances have dictated the approach of this book. It is not a do-it-yourself guide, but is intended to supplement (not replace) an experienced dive guide. Many more sites are now available. All the popular ones are described, as well as some of the lesser known ones. The emphasis is on what will be seen underwater rather than on how to get there. The reader can use this book to plan a trip and make decisions where to go. At the dive center, choices of sites can be made and discussed with the guide. If two centers are offering different trips, an informed choice between them can be made from the descriptions presented here. For a trip scheduled to a specific spot, the site can be previewed in these pages.

Although the Red Sea is no longer considered a frontier, many of the dive centers and hotels have not been around long enough to establish a track record. Even in more developed resort areas, diving is a volatile business and operators sometimes open and close in short

The Nile is Egypt's lifeline. At sunset, a felluca sails south with the prevailing wind. (photo by Mia Tegner)

order. Nothing dates a book or compromises its credibility as quickly as the inclusion of hotels, restaurants or operations that have gone out of business. Therefore, specific hotels and dive centers are not included in the text.

General travel guides are usually updated every year or two. No diving guidebook can keep up with changes in room rates, airfares, restaurant prices, or currency regulations. All those items may be found in the travel guides, a selection of which is listed in Chapter II. It is suggested that the reader buy one as a topside supplement to this book for current information on travel in Egypt. This is especially important if you plan to spend a week or so seeing the archaeological sites.

Some of the highlights of travel in Egypt are presented in Chapter IX. If you have only a day or two to spend in Cairo, the information contained there will probably be sufficient. But it would be a shame to see the Red Sea and miss Egypt. Chapter IX tells what you would be missing, and hopefully will motivate you to explore the country in greater depth. Additional references in the Bibliography offer further information.

To gather data for this book, I spent over nine months in Egypt, spread out over five summers between 1982 and 1988. I made close to 300 dives in the Red Sea, from Eilat to the southern Egyptian coast, covering nearly all the sites mentioned in the text. Although some sites were visited over a dozen times, it isn't possible to really know them with such short exposure, during only one season of the year. Fortunately, guides and other active divers were willing to share their knowledge; without their contributions this book would not have been possible. Their names appear on the acknowledgement page. Whenever possible, two or more persons were interviewed about each site, so their descriptions could be compared with each other and with my own observations.

The scope of this book is limited to the diving in the Egyptian Red Sea. It does not include sites in Israel, Jordan, Saudi Arabia or Sudan, although these countries also offer Red Sea diving. Egyptian sites have been divided into three areas: Sinai, Hurghada, and the South. There is some overlap; for example, Ras Muhammed can be dived while based in Sinai or Hurghada. The description of each site is located in the area from which it is most easily accessible. Dive sites are covered in Chapters V (Sinai), VI (Hurghada), and VII (The South). Anyone going to the Red Sea for the first time should concentrate on either Sinai or Hurghada, perhaps visiting the alternate area on a second trip. Save the South for the third time, after you have seen the areas which are easily accessible. The South represents the Egyptian Red Sea's ultimate frontier experience for the hard-core diver who doesn't mind some discomfort and hardship.

Chapter II covers the basic facts you will need to know when planning your trip, and how to get around and get along when you are there. Be sure to read the section on the Egyptian people. It will help you to understand the country and its culture, and adjust to its ways to gain more from your travels.

The oceanography and biology of the Red Sea is fascinating. Many questions will be raised by the things which you will observe. Some of them are answered in Chapter III, written by Dr. Mia Tegner, a marine biologist from Scripps Institution of Oceanography.

Far better qualified to write it than I am, she presents a wealth of information in a concise, readable manner.

Chapter VIII, Night Diving, covers a specialized aspect of Red Sea diving which most divers will want to experience. Chapter IV describes some of the more common creatures and their behavior, from the standpoint of a sport diver. Tips on finding and photographing them are included.

There are two appendices. The first is a glossary of diving terms in Arabic. Although most diving guides speak excellent English, Arabic could be valuable for communicating with boat crews. The second is a bibliography of publications related to Egypt and the Red Sea.

Sidebars are inserted throughout the book to present information that doesn't fit directly into the text, but is nonetheless pertinent. It is our hope that this volume will be helpful in planning and carrying out your journey to the Egyptian Red Sea.

Arches and coral pillars give The Temple its name. Note the lionfish, upside down at top center.

Chapter I

Reflections on a Blue Sea

"The Red Sea is a corridor of marvels...The happiest hours of my diving experience have been spent there."
Jacques Cousteau

At the edge of the Egyptian desert, beneath the sapphire blue waters of the Red Sea, lies a submerged oasis of incredibly rich and beautiful marine life. Ever since the early explorations of Hans Hass and Jacques Cousteau, this underwater paradise has been a prime destination of knowledgeable divers from all over the world.

What is it about this desert sea that has captured the imagination of people who have seen the best that the underwater world has to offer? Perhaps it is the warm, crystalline water with its profusion of brilliantly- hued invertebrates and reef fish. The vibrant colors make most other tropical seas seem dull and monochromatic by comparison. There are big fish that remind a diver he is only a visitor in their realm: manta rays, groupers, Napoleon Wrasses, and even an occasional shark. Sheer walls of the fringing reefs often begin at the surface and drop off into the indigo blue of infinity. There are enough sunken ships to keep an avid wreck diver occupied for years. Some

The Temple of Abu Simbel was dismantled and moved to higher ground in the 60s, to save it from the floodwaters of the Aswan High Dam.

The ornate interior of the Mohammed Ali Mosque impresses tourists, but draws scorn from architectural purists.

remote islands, rising from the depths, are visited by fewer than 50 persons a year.

Diving areas in other parts of the world may also offer some of these elements; only a handful have all of them. But the Red Sea has even more. Its gateway is Egypt, the historic land where civilization began. Her ancient artifacts and monuments have been preserved up to 5,000 years by the harsh desert environment. The Pyramids, the Sphinx, the tombs of the Pharaohs, medieval fortresses, mosques, and monasteries are all there for the traveler to see and experience.

Egypt is the crossroads of the world. For over 2,000 years after the pharaoanic era, it was controlled by foreign powers. The Greeks, the Romans, the Mamelukes, the Turks, the French, and the British all conquered the land at one time or another. And each power, in turn, has left something of its culture behind.

Today's Egypt is a land of contrasts. As the ancient pyramids greet another sunrise (they have already seen over 1,600,000 of them) the sounds and smells of the city rise from below. Tourists receive their wake-up calls in luxurious, air-conditioned, five-star hotels while the buzzing of the flies awakens the poor in Cairo's slums. From a minaret, the muezzin's call to prayer is heard above the cacophony of automobile horns. Women in the cities wear the latest Paris fashions while those in the villages still cover their heads with the traditional black shawls. In the desert, high-tech oil rigs pump their precious liquid from the ground while cattle-driven water wheels

Cairo comes alive at night. This view is toward Gezirah Island, with the Cairo Tower.

irrigate the fields along the banks of the Nile. In Sinai villages, some Bedouins ride camels while others drive Mercedes.

It is all there in Egypt: the motorized bustle of Africa's largest city, the fields along the Nile still farmed virtually the way they were in the days of the Pharaohs, and the azure crystalline waters of the Red Sea. Many of the world's top diving areas offer little else once you leave the water. The Red Sea also offers Egypt, its topside scenes matching the splendor of its underwater environment.

For 15 years, the gateway for divers traveling to the Red Sea had been through Israel. After gaining control of the Sinai Peninsula in the 1967 war, Israelis began to develop its potential. They drilled for oil on land and sea, mined its rocks for minerals, built kibbutzes, and opened diving centers along its shores.

The diving resorts were located at Naama Bay, just north of Sharm El Sheikh near the southern tip of the peninsula, and at Dahab and Nuweiba in the Gulf of Aquaba. For 15 years as travelers returned home, their books, articles, films and word of mouth conveyed the impression that Israel's area of Red Sea was the ultimate diving paradise. Israel's area was, in fact, limited to the western shores of the Gulf of Aqaba, comprising less than five percent of the total shoreline. But, as far as most traveling divers were concerned, the Gulf of Aqaba *was* the Red Sea.

That came to an end on April 25, 1982, when the last section of the Sinai was returned to Egyptian control under the terms of the Camp David Peace Accords. As a result the western Red Sea, from Sinai to the Sudanese border, was united under one flag. The immediate reaction in the diving community was one of concern.

Dating back some 4,000 years, the Sphinx and Pyramids are the only survivors of the Seven Wonders of the Ancient World.

19

Would the dive sites be accessible under Egyptian control? Would the infrastructure, facilities, and equipment be there to support diving operations? Would the Egyptians protect the environment? The country had little sport diving background or tradition, yet it had a long history of tourism, and was seeking new venues. The government was looking for ways to lure tourists back to Egypt after they had seen the Pyramids and the temples along the Nile. It realized that the beaches and reefs of the Red Sea might be that lure.

THE EGYPTIAN RED SEA TODAY

Egypt today has over 800 miles of coastline on the Red Sea. Some of it, along the Gulf of Suez, is not worth diving because its shallow and sandy bottom inhibits visbility and coral growth. The southern area, near the Sudan border, is so isolated and undeveloped that a diving trip there must be a fully equipped expedition. This leaves two easily accessible diving regions: the Sinai peninsula, and the mainland from the lower Gulf of Suez to the port of Safaga. The primary location of the diving centers are Naama Bay in Sinai and the city of Hurghada on the mainland.

Under the Camp David agreement, Israeli owners were paid for the businesses they gave up when the Sinai was returned to Egyptian control. As a result of this settlement, a joint-venture company was formed to run the properties at Dahab, Nuweiba, and Naama Bay. The centers had been run by foreign contractors under the Israelis; many of them were persuaded to remain and run them under the new regime.

Because of the uncertainty, diving tourism fell off in the first two years. That may have been a blessing in disguise. With less diver pressure, the reefs and walls had time to heal the inadvertent wounds caused by thousands of sets of fins belonging to divers who were loving them to death. Rumors of dynamiting and uncontrolled spearfishing turned out to be false. Ras Muhammed was declared a national park, thanks largely to lobbying efforts spearheaded by Dr. Eugenie Clark. Spearfishing and coral collecting have been banned since 1977 throughout the Egyptian Red Sea. Although enforcement

THE RED SEA AT A GLANCE

Length:	Approximately 1,200 miles
Width:	90 to 190 miles
Area:	169,000 square miles
Gulf of Aqaba:	98 miles long, 1,800 meters greatest depth
Gulf of Suez:	75 miles long, 73 meters greatest depth
Average depth of Red Sea:	491 meters
Maximum depth:	2,500 meters
Egyptian Red Sea:	550 miles long, 825 miles of coastline
Tide:	Semidiurnal, .5 meters in north & south end, 0 at Port Sudan and Jeddah
Average water temperatures:	(Gulf of Suez) 80 in Aug., 66 in Feb. (Hot saline deeps) 140 degrees
Number of coral species: Over 100	
Number of fish species: Over 1,000	
Countries bordering on the Red Sea:	Egypt, Israel, Jordan, Saudi Arabia, Yemen, South Yemen, Djibouti, Ethiopia, Sudan

is spotty at best, the preservation ethic is at work.

Today, dive tourism has grown to the level of earlier times. Private companies have constructed three new hotels and dive centers in Naama Bay, and more are planned. Larger, more luxurious boats are now available, both for day trips and live-aboard diving. Direct charter flights from Europe to Sinai began in 1987. Naama Bay had been a frontier town, but its pace of change is accelerating to meet the future.

Most of the diving in Sinai is wall diving, done along the fringing reefs bordering the eastern coast of the peninsula. Many sites are accessible from land. Diving is also done on the Tiran Islands and the submerged reefs which form the Straits of Tiran. Since the Sinai

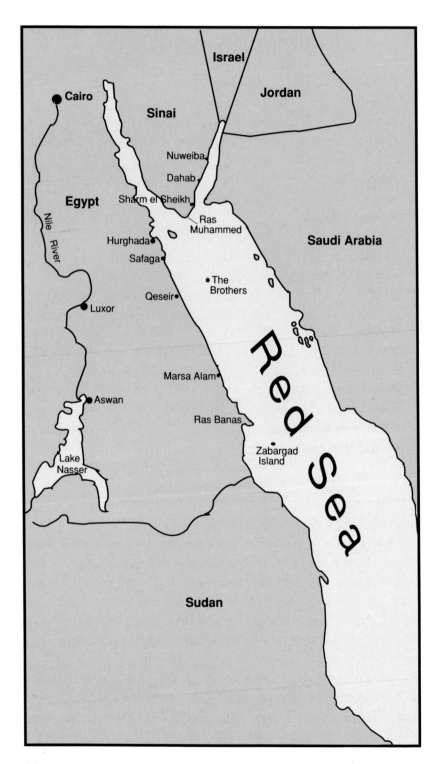

Israel

Cairo

Jordan

Sinai

Nuweiba

Dahab

Egypt   Sharm el Sheikh

Nile River

Ras Muhammed

Saudi Arabia

Hurghada

Safaga

• The Brothers

Qeseir•

Luxor

Red Sea

Marsa Alam•

Aswan

Ras Banas

Lake Nasser

Zabargad Island

Sudan

coast drops steeply into very deep water, there are few other offshore reefs.

The first dive center in the Red Sea was opened in the mainland town of Hurghada by a German couple, Peter and Helga Kopp, in the early 1960s. European divers, especially those from Germany and Italy, made Hurghada a major diving resort center well before anything had been developed in Sinai. This lasted until the 1967 war, when the city was declared a combat zone and was closed to all foreigners. The ban lasted eight years. So while sport diving thrived under the Israelis in Sinai, it died completely in Hurghada. When tensions began to ease in 1975, President Anwar Sadat reopened the area. Kopp, unfortunately, was no longer around. He was killed in an automobile accident in Europe.

Hurghada today still attracts many European divers, but Americans have also discovered the mainland. Like Naama Bay, its coastline has undergone major development in the mid 80s, transforming the small fishing village into a major seaside resort. Over a dozen dive centers are located there.

The wreck of the Aida, *at the Brothers Islands, is decorated with a lush growth of soft corals.*

The dive sites around Hurghada are located on small islands and offshore reefs. Nearly all of them are accessible only by boat. The reefs are especially interesting, rising from relatively deep water and offering wall dives, reef scenery, and pelagic fish. Located south of the Suez Gulf near the busy Red Sea shipping channel, there are many diveable shipwrecks.

DIVING HISTORY

The first person to dive the Red Sea and tell the world about it was the Austrian pioneer, Dr. Hans Hass. A PhD in zoology, he had become an internationally renowned underwater moviemaker in 1939, filming sharks in the Caribbean while using rebreathers for his air supply. This occurred four years before Jacques Cousteau and Emile Gagnan invented scuba as we know it. After losing nearly everything in World War II, Haas was seeking a way to regain his fortune and his reputation. The unexplored underwater world of the Red Sea provided that opportunity.

Hass borrowed money, secured the necessary permits, and set off alone for Port Sudan in the autumn of 1949. The heaviest item in his luggage was 66 pounds of caustic soda, the carbon dioxide absorbent used in his rebreathing apparatus. In two months of solitary diving, Hass shot over 1,500 photographs, using housings he had designed and built for Leica and Rolleiflex. They included pictures of sharks and manta rays which look sensational even by today's standards. At that time, most people believed mantas were man-eaters. Hass filmed the "devil rays" swimming directly at the camera, tiny pilot fish inside their open mouths. Although shot in black and white, Hass' photographs of reef creatures, the wreck of the Italian ship *Umbria*, and sharks and rays have the impact of living history. When you realize that he didn't have the advantages of today's sophisticated optics, viewing systems and strobes, the scope of his achievement really hits home. The story of his adventures was published in 1952 under the title *Manta: Under the Red Sea with Spear and Camera*.

Hass returned to Port Sudan in May, 1950 accompanied by a film crew and a beautiful assistant, Lotte, who later became his wife. This

24

Once the most popular wreck in the Red Sea, the Jolanda *has slipped off its shallow reef. She now rests in 300 feet of water.*

time they made a motion picture, "Under the Red Sea," which became the commercial success he had sought. Its sensational footage included the first pictures ever taken of a whale shark underwater. Profits from the movie were used to build a 143-foot three-masted schooner, *Xarifa* (meaning Charming Lady in Arabic), which was used for their subsequent diving expeditions.

Jacques Cousteau arrived in the Red Sea on *Calypso* in 1951, a year after Hass had left. His early voyages there are recounted in his classic book, *The Silent World*, and in his Academy Award winning movie of the same name. Most of Cousteau's diving was done near Port Sudan and on the shallow reefs of the Saudi Arabian coast. However, he did make a stop at The Brothers in the Egyptian Red Sea, describing the shark activity there and taking some of the islets' profuse black coral. Those were innocent years, before we realized the magnitude of man's impact on the marine environment.

Cousteau returned to the Red Sea many times, ranking it his

Egypt at a Glance

Area:	386,662 square miles
Coastline:	565 miles on the Mediterranean
	825 miles on the Red Sea
Highest elevation:	8,652 feet above sea level, St. Catherine's Mountain
Lowest elevation:	436 feet below sea level, Qattara Depression
Population:	50,000,000
Capitol:	Cairo
Other major ciies:	Alexandria, Suez, Aswan, Luxor
Religion:	Sunni Muslim and Coptic Orthodox
Language:	Arabic, English
Government:	Republic
Literacy:	44%
Life expectancy:	57 years
Per capita income:	$686
Industries:	Oil, textiles, tourism
Export crops:	Cotton, rice

favorite diving area in the world. His first man-in-the-sea project took place in the waters off Port Sudan. The remains of the old Conshelf habitat are still there and can be visited by sport divers. Cousteau's books, articles and films perhaps did more than anything else to make the fledgling diving community aware of the wonders that lay below the surface of the Red Sea.

About the time Hass arrived in Port Sudan, a young American marine biologist, Eugenie Clark, received a Fullbright Grant to do research under the renowned Egyptian scientist, Dr. H. A. F. Gohar. His laboratory was located in a small fishing village on the Red Sea called Ghardaka. (Today the town is usually referred to as Hurghada, an English corruption of the original name.)

Equipped only with primitive snorkeling equipment, she and Gohar studied the fishes of the local reefs. For Clark, it was the beginning of a 35-year love affair with the Red Sea which continues to the present day.

Dr. Clark has returned many times since then, working with both Israelis and Egyptians. She discovered a shark repelling substance secreted by the Moses Sole, a small flatfish found on sandy bottoms. She has also described the activities of flashlight fish, garden eels, sharks, and many of the Red Sea reef fish. When it became evident that the Sinai would be returned to Egypt, she convinced Anwar Sadat that Ras Muhammed should receive the same protection it had had under Israel. He was killed before anything could be done, but President Hosni Mubarak and the Egyptian Parliament declared the region a national park and wildlife reserve in 1983.

Sport diving in the Red Sea began in the 1950s when Greeks and Italians working for oil and mining companies began skin diving along the coast. Their primary interest was spearfishing, and they exacted a heavy toll on the population of large groupers around the reefs. It wasn't until after the reopening of Hurghada in 1975 that concern was voiced about unchecked spearfishing. Big fish had returned to the reefs during the eight years the area had been closed, but now the slaughter was beginning again. Dive guides were the first to voice opposition; tourists and fishermen joined in. Finally in 1977, the government placed a total ban on spearfishing in the Egyptian Red Sea.

Hans Hass, then in his late 60s, recently returned to dive with Rudi Kneip out of Hurghada. He bemoaned the state of the Red Sea today, contrasting it with what he had seen 35 years ago. "The fish are all gone," he said. "In the old days I used to have to beat them off, now I can't approach them." He went on to complain that all the corals are broken and everything is bare.

It all depends on your perspective. My first visit to the Red Sea came 32 years after that of Hans Hass, and I considered it the richest, most colorful place I had ever dived. Few people were fortunate enough to dive the Red Sea in its virgin days. Hass' view compares to the Vikings' first look at the forests of North America. The early pioneers really did see the best of the underwater world, before there were resorts and dive centers and live-aboard boats. Only when we leave those comforts behind and travel to remote areas can we get an idea of the way it was.

Framed by an overhang and a soft coral, a diver descends Pinky's Wall.

Chapter 2

A survival Guide on Land and Sea

PLANNING A TRIP

Several excellent guidebooks are available which thoroughly cover hotels, restaurants, travel and border formalities, as well as places to go and things to see. Most of them are updated annually. Although someone going to Egypt just to dive could get by with this book alone, I recommend the purchase of one or more of the books listed below to supplement it for land travel.

Fodor's Egypt by Kay Showker, distributed by David McKay Company, New York. Updated annually. One of a well known series of guides, this one is well organized and covers the upper to middle price ranges of accommodations, food and transportation. Mostly devoted to Cairo and vicinity, it also discusses the archaeological sites in Upper Egypt and Alexandria.

Frommer's Dollarwise Guide to Egypt by Nancy McGrath, Simon & Schuster, New York. Updated biannually. Another popular guidebook, this one concentrates on accommodations and meals in the middle price range, although all levels are covered.

Let's Go: Israel and Egypt St. Martin's Press, New York. Updated annually. Written by and for students by Harvard Student Agencies, this represents the lower end of the spectrum in terms of price ranges. Devoted to a more adventurous style of travel, half of its pages are about Egypt with lots of practical information on getting about on your own. It even has a couple of pages on diving the Red Sea.

Travelaid Guide to Egypt by Michael von Haag, Travelaid Publishing, London. Updated annually. Not readily available in the United States, we picked this up in Egypt. It represents a point of view between the extremes of price ranges, and is the most readable of the group. The author includes a lot of personal experience and opinion, which raises it above the level of most guidebooks. It is especially good on history and archaeological sites.

Current information is also available from the EGYPTIAN GOVERNMENT TOURIST OFFICES. In the United States they are located at 630 Fifth Avenue, New York, NY 10111 (telephone

[212] 246-6960); and 323 Geary Street, San Francisco, CA 94102 (telephone [415] 781-7676). In Canada, the address is Place Bonaventure, Frontenac 40, PO Box 304, Montreal, Quebec H5A 1B4 (telephone [514] 861-4420). These offices offer information only. A visa is required for tourists, which can be obtained from the EGYPTIAN CONSULATES. Their locations in the USA are: 2310 Decatur Pl NW, Washington, DC 20008; 1110 Second Avenue, New York, NY 10022; and 3001 Pacific Avenue, San Francisco, CA 94115. There are also Egyptian consulates in Chicago and Houston. In Canada the address is 3754 Cote de Nieges, Montreal, and 454 Lurier Avenue NE, Ottawa. When entering Egypt from other countries, check on current regulations at the local Egyptian Consulate. A visa will shorten immigration formalities at the airport. However, they can be obtained upon arrival if necessary.

SHOTS AND MEDICATIONS

No shots are currently required for traveling to Egypt. Malaria is not a problem because of the dry climate. Sanitation is not quite up to the standards of Europe and America, except in the better class tourist establishments. However, aside from minor intestinal upsets, a visitor shouldn't have to worry about any health problems. A gamma globulin shot is recommended to enhance general immunity. It can reduce chances of contracting hepatitis, although nothing is failsafe against that disease. The shot is effective for about eight weeks, giving your body's immune system a chance to protect itself against germs it hasn't encountered before. It even seems to reduce the incidence and severity of traveler's diarrhea. Just to be sure, though, bring along Lomotil or its equivalent. (See sidebar: Gippy Tummy) Although pharmacies in the large cities carry a full line of drugs and medications, it is advisable to bring along your own prescription medicines. For diving, don't forget a decongestant and a motion sickness preventative if you are susceptible. A multiple vitamin is a good idea whenever you are subjected to a different diet, with perhaps fewer fruits and vegetables than you are used to. Sunscreen and aspirin are a couple of often overlooked but necessary items in personal first aid kits.

Cairo's skyline is dominated by the minarets of its mosques.

GETTING THERE

Airline fares to Egypt vary considerably with the carrier, the time of year you go, and how far in advance the ticket is purchased. An experienced travel agent can be very helpful in obtaining the best possible price. Be sure to check on current regulations regarding baggage allowances. Judicious packing can avoid or minimize excess baggage charges. A large ice chest equipped with a padlock is excellent for transporting camera gear. Clothes can be used for padding instead of foam, then be transferred to a soft bag when reaching your destination. At the dive site, the ice chest will hold a great deal of equipment in addition to cameras, and doubles as a bench or table.

ARRIVAL

Foreign travel agents usually contract with small local agencies in Cairo who will have an airport representative "meet and assist" you when you arrive. The airport agent will help you through immigration. Even customs inspectors will usually pass you with barely a cursory glance. Occasionally, however, a zealous type will enforce the law to the letter. He is concerned that you might sell your diving or camera equipment in Egypt, circumventing the country's import duties. He may record the serial numbers on your passport, and you will have to produce the items when leaving the country or pay a fine. Inspectors are especially suspicious of video cameras because they are in strong demand in Egypt. Usually, though, the airport agent will help you through customs with no hassles.

You will be extremely grateful to your newfound friend, but will never see him again. The airport agent is licensed to do just what he did for you and nothing more. He usually meets several visitors every day. But that doesn't diminish his value. As you load your gear in the taxi, your fellow travelers will still be in line waiting to get through customs. Give him some baksheesh; he deserves it.

Without an airport agent, just prepared to stand in lines for a while longer. You will have to answer some questions at immigration, and undergo a more thorough customs inspection. But aside from the helpless feeling of being in a strange new environment, entry procedures in Egypt are no more difficult than those in many of the western democracies.

Within a week of your arrival, your passport must be registered. This will be done by the hotel. The clerk at the registration desk will request your passport when you check in, and keep it overnight to get the proper stamp. If you are heading straight to a diving area, the hotel clerk at your destination can do it. If the passport is not registered within seven days, you could be subject to a fine.

A major expansion of the Cairo airport was completed in 1986, including a new international terminal. In addition, charter flights from Europe land directly in Hurghada and Sharm El Sheikh. The result has been to ease entry procedures for traveling divers.

CURRENCY

Egypt formerly had a fixed currency rate, with the pound (comprised of 100 piastres and abbreviated LE) pegged artificially high against the dollar. As a result a thriving black market developed,

BAKSHEESH

The word baksheesh comes from the Turkish, and means "Share the wealth." It is often the first word a tourist learns in Egypt. Baksheesh can take the form of a tip, a handout, or a bribe. The biggest questions are when and how much.

Sometimes it seems that everyone expects baksheesh. Tipping in Egypt is more prevalent than in most western countries. But people are satisfied with less. While a New York city cabbie would look down his nose at a 15 percent tip, his Cairo counterpart will be happy with a pound or two. Many necessities, such as bread and public transportation, are heavily subsidized in Egypt. A 25 piastre tip buys a lot of bread. Small bills, in 25 and 50 piastre denominations, may seem like a nuisance when you receive them in change. But it's good to have them available in a pocket for baksheesh purposes.

The best advice is to pay according to the service performed. A bellhop who lugged 150 pounds of diving and camera gear to your room rates more than the doorman who hailed a cab.

At archaeological sites, people sometimes offer to take you to a better vantage point or to areas normally closed to the public. Sometimes they will point out a picture spot or an erotic carving. If you aren't interested, tell them "la" (no), or if they are persistent, "imshee" (go away). But if you really want that closeup of the Sphinx, or the high level view at Karnak, or the shot of the fertility god's erection, take him up on it and pay according to what it's worth. 50 piastres is plenty. Don't feel guilty if they act dissatisfied; it's part of the game.

Beggars are not as prevalent or as pushy in Egypt as in some other countries. Use your own judgment. Natives are often more generous than tourists, especially on Muslim holy days.

where the exchange rate on the street was far more favorable than that in the banks. Early in 1987, the government floated the pound. The black market was dead within a month, and foreign currency began to flow once again into Egyptian banks. For the traveller this has provided a double benefit. First, the risks of obtaining counterfeit money from the black market are gone. Second, prices have remained fairly stable, making your foreign currency go much further. Consequently, Egypt has been transformed from an expensive country for tourists into a genuine travel bargain.

GETTING AROUND IN CAIRO

Upon arrival, all you will want to do is find your hotel and recover from jet lag. Egyptian time is seven hours ahead of New York's standard time and ten ahead of Los Angeles. Taxis are easy to get at the airport; the airport agent will have one arranged for you. Even if you arrived on your own, the drivers will be hustling you; you won't have to look for them. Don't expect the meter to be running, most are broken or disconnected.

But despite the higher prices charged tourists, Cairo taxis are a bargain. The price should be agreed upon ahead of time, and a tip is customary, especially if the driver has to haul diving gear. (See sidebar: Baksheesh). The drive will be your first real adventure in Egypt

If you signed up for a package tour, a guide will

Vendors ply their wares on the old market street in Luxor. Most people here wear the traditional galabiyahs instead of the western clothing of Cairo residents.

36

pick you up at the hotel each day in a private car or van. If on your own, private taxis are the easiest way to go. Ask the hotel doorman about the typical fare to your destination. That will provide a sound basis for bargaining with the cab driver. (See sidebar: Bargaining, Chapter IX) A cheaper alternative is the jitney taxi, which is shared with other passengers heading in the same general direction. They are painted black and white; sometimes they also serve as private taxis. If you aren't in a hurry and don't mind a more circuitous route, the jitneys are about fifty percent cheaper.

GETTING AROUND IN EGYPT

A traveler in Egypt will have the opportunity to ride in a wide variety of conveyances, from camels and horsedrawn carriages to taxis, buses, and trolleys, to fishing boats and sailing ships, to propeller-driven planes and jets.

The national airline, Egypt Air, flies on a regular schedule between Cairo and Hurghada, Luxor and Aswan. Its subsidiary, Air Sinai, goes to Sharm El Sheikh. Flights are usually packed, so book well in advance and reconfirm your reservations.

Air-conditioned buses travel on a regular schedule between most tourist destinations. Although they are slower than flying, the seats are wider and more comfortable. Trains with sleeping compartments run overnight between Cairo, Luxor and Aswan. Giant cruise ships, with all the amenities of a floating

Ramses II never imagined his statue would someday look out over 20th century traffic jams.

37

CAIRO TRAFFIC

The first ride in Cairo traffic might seem like motorized anarchy to passengers who are used to smooth flowing freeways or autobahns. Consider this. Lane lines are often ignored; a street will accommodate as many cars abreast as will fit. You are usually so close you could shake the hand of the person in the car next to you. More horns are honked in one block of driving in Cairo than you would hear in a month back home. It's said if the horn stops working it wouldn't be possible to drive the car.

Accidents are so common they are just called "bumps." Usually the drivers don't even stop to survey the damage. They just shout a few choice Arabic expletives at each other and proceed on their way.

Few persons ever get hurt because the cars are moving so slowly. But crossing a street downtown is like the running of the bulls at Pamplona. Pedestrians don't carry the shield of protection they are used to in the west; at times they feel like targets.

Traffic has improved recently with the construction of new overpasses. And an improved, computerized telephone service no longer makes it necessary to conduct all business in person. This has resulted in a decrease in the number of cars on the road. Generally traffic moves more smoothly and rapidly than before, but near gridlock conditions are still present in some parts of the city. The basic problem is that there are still too many automobiles. Driving through downtown Cairo on a business day can make rush hour on the Santa Monica Freeway seem like the Indianapolis 500.

Needless to say, this isn't the place to rent a vehicle. Fortunately, taxis and hired cars with drivers are quite reasonable and, if you're not in a hurry, it's best to leave the driving to them. If you are in a hurry, malesh (see sidebar: IBM).

Thoroughly intimidated, I swore early on I would never drive in Cairo. But one day a friend consumed half a bottle of scotch in a half hour. Weaving unsteadily, he declared he was ready to drive me home. No way! At that point I figured it was better to take my chances behind the wheel. The trip that followed took me back to earlier days on a learner's permit. From the passenger's seat, my friend gave directions and advice, smug in the knowledge that as drunk as he was, he could have done a better job. It seemed everyone was either honking at me or trying to squeeze me out of the lane. We made it without a bump, but with lots of close calls and anxiety.

I never drove in Cairo again. I'd rather face a shark any time.

hotel, ply the waters of the Nile from Cairo to Aswan, with stops at points of interest along the way. If none of the schedules coincide with yours, a car and driver can be hired to take you where you want to go, whenever you want to leave.

HOTELS

Many of the large international chains have hotels in Cairo, including Sheraton, Hilton, Marriott, Hyatt, Intercontinental, and Meridien. Reservations are recommended, and can be made by telex from any of their sister hotels worldwide. Even if you are staying in

The bustling city of Cairo is home to some 15 million people. This view is from the Gezirah Sheraton.

Cairo only a day or two, it will be worthwhile to stay in one of those establishments. For the first-time traveler to the Middle East, it will ease the transition to a different way of life and offer a haven in which to sleep off some jet lag. The five-star hotels in Cairo are essentially like those at home with air-conditioned rooms, cable TV and fine restaurants; but prices are about 25 percent lower than their western counterparts.

FOOD AND DRINK

One of the delights of travel is to experience exotic foreign foods. Egypt has more than its share, combining native dishes with those of Greece, Turkey and other nations which have occupied the country through the centuries. But don't expect to find authentic Egyptian food featured at the hotels. It's there, but you might have to look hard for it. Hotel restaurants generally offer the kind of continental cuisine expected by a cosmopolitan clientele. There are many excellent restaurants in Cairo which offer native food. Ask for recommendations.

Egyptian cooking is primarily Middle Eastern, with a strong European influence. Devotees of Greek cooking will find several familiar items on Egyptian menus. Gebna beida is a white cheese, similar to feta, which is mixed with tomatoes, onions and cucumbers in salads, or is eaten in sandwiches. It is a staple among fishermen in the Red Sea because its high salt content retards spoilage. The taste is a bit too salty for western palates, but it's fine when used sparingly in salads and sandwiches. The most common type of bread is aish baladi, a type of pita made with coarse whole wheat flour. Local fast food establishments often serve it filled with shawerma, which we would recognize as the Greek grilled lamb dish, gyros.

The national staple is a bean dish called fool, made from fava beans. Egyptians eat it for breakfast, as well as a main dish or a side course for other meals. The best I had was made by Bedouins in Sinai, who mixed it with tomatoes, onions, and spices for a delicious dinner under a zillion desert stars. Fool is sometimes mashed, spiced and fried in oil as patties. In this form it is called taamiya; middle eastern food buffs would recognize it as felafel. Eaten as a sandwich

Many small town markets, like this one in Quesir, have been in the same location for over a thousand years.

in aish baladi, with tomatoes and onions added, it makes an excellent lunch.

Although many Middle Eastern specialties are acquired tastes, nearly everyone will like kebab and kufta. Kebab consists of marinated chunks of lamb roasted on a skewer over an open fire. Kufta is spiced ground lamb formed into finger patties, and cooked the same way. They are often served together.

Tahina is a dip made from ground sesame seeds, lemon and spices. An all-purpose food, it can be used as a salad dressing, on sandwiches, or as a dip with pieces of aish.

Lunches on the Red Sea will often consist of samak, or fried fresh fish. It doesn't really matter what kind of fish it is, because it all tastes good when it was swimming just a couple of hours before. The side dish is usually rice, boiled in a broth with onions and spices. It tastes good and really fills the empty spaces on dive boat trips, although after about a week of the same thing you start craving a Big Mac. McDonald's hasn't made it to Egypt yet but for those who can't wean

GIPPY TUMMY

The dread of any traveler is an intestinal upset known by various names throughout the world. In Egypt it's the Tutankhamen Trot, or Ramses' Revenge, or Gippy Tummy. The easiest way to spot a tourist in Egypt is by a bottle of mineral water constantly clutched to the breast in the fervent hope that this will ward off evil spirits.

The Egyptian version of traveler's diarrhea is a mild form which usually runs its course within two to three days. It's not debilitating as is the case in some other areas of the world. You shouldn't miss any diving time from its effects. And finally, it's all right to drink the water. Nile water is so heavily chlorinated that only the hardiest bug could survive. Of course, it doesn't taste very good; perhaps that's a reason to opt for other liquids.

Many people staying in Egypt for any length of time begin drinking local water from the first day on. That puts the problem behind them, and allows the body to build up its immune response against future attacks.

If you are especially susceptible, some common sense precautions will help you minimize the uncomfortable effects. Be wary of street food and stick to fruits and vegetables that can be peeled. But don't be paranoid or you'll miss the exotic cuisine. If you do come down with Gippy Tummy, don't panic. Pepto Bismol or a similar over-the-counter remedy usually does the job in mild cases. Tablets are easier to carry than the liquid. For severe attacks, Lomotil is usually effective. That's a prescription item, so see your doctor before you leave. He or she may prescribe something even more potent.

Don't forget that diarrhea dehydrates you, and that can become serious in a hot climate. Drink lots of fluids but avoid fruit juices, carbonated beverages, and alcohol. Finally, if symptoms persist for more than three days or are accompanied by fever, see a doctor.

themselves away from American food, there are a couple of Kentucky Fried Chicken places in Cairo, along with several Wimpys, a British hamburger chain.

Although the Muslim religion frowns on liquor, there are no qualms about selling it at the hotel bars. The national beer, Stella, is uneven in quality with individual bottles ranging from good to awful. Sometimes it leaves the plant without proper aging. Imported beers, once impossible to obtain except at foreign embassies and military installations, are beginning to be more readily available, but at a premium price. Mixed drinks tend to favor gin and scotch, probably due to the British influence.

EGYPTIANS

Islam has had a bad press around the world in the past few years. Americans especially seem to throw an ideological blanket over the entire Middle East, equating all Muslims with Khoumeni and Kadafi. When there are troubles in Lebanon, people think that Egypt or Saudi Arabia will be the next to go up in flames. Granted, virtually nothing happens in the world these days that won't have repercussions somewhere else. But the Middle East is far from a monolithic area. There are republics and dictatorships, conservatives and liberals, countries that hate the west and countries that love the west.

Egypt falls into the second category. When you travel to a tourist attraction, you will be surrounded by vendors and hawkers, discovering immediately that the people love your dollars. But there is more to it than that. Their "welcome" is from the heart as well as from the pocketbook. Of course, Egypt has its problems. They are basically the same as many third world countries: overpopulation and poverty. No matter how much you have traveled, you will be affected by the slums of Cairo. Yet the people cope and make the best of their lot in life. And they do it with a very low crime rate, and without obvious envy of wealthy (by their standards) tourists. They are among the most generous and hospitable people in the world.

But first impressions can be disturbing. At the airport, the visitor is first confronted by the bureaucracy, a legacy of 76 years of British rule. A female, especially when traveling alone, will be the subject of stares and comments as the men play their macho role. At the tourist sites, scores of vendors, camel drivers, and a few beggars clamor for your attention and your money. The noise, the dust, the congestion, the perpetual construction and destruction of streets and buildings are powerful impressions. Many tourists never venture out from their protected enclaves to look beyond the surface, and fail to encounter the real Egypt.

The real Egypt is found in its people. And, whether they are true believers or casual observers, their attitudes and customs are shaped by their Islamic faith. About 90 percent of Egyptians are Sunni Muslims. Another 10 percent belong to the Coptic church, one of the earliest Christian sects.

Muslims believe in one God, called "Allah" in Arabic. The religion was founded by the prophet Mohammed in the seventh century; its holy book is the Koran. The Five Pillars of Islam are the Ramadan fast, giving alms to the poor, the pilgrimage to Mecca, daily prayers, and the recognition of only one God. Devout Muslims pray five times a day, prostrating themselves on a carpet and facing the holy city, Mecca.

Cairo's skyline is dominated by the minarets of its many mosques. Since a mosque is a house of worship, visitors should remain quiet and reverent, especially when prayers are going on. When entering, it is customary to remove your shoes. Men should wear long pants, women should be dressed modestly. Avoid walking between the worshippers and the eastern wall, which they will be facing. Friday is the Muslim sabbath, a day for prayer. (Weekends in Egypt are Friday and Saturday. Offices will be closed, but most stores remain open.) Schedule your visit to avoid mid-day services.

It's hard not to be impressed, because the soaring architecture and the intricate decorations of a mosque inspire a sense of awe. Inside, one can begin to understand the hold that Islam has on its people.

Drinking alcoholic beverages and eating pork are forbidden. Although many Muslims break these taboos, they are widely observed. In the old days, stealing was punished by chopping off the offender's right hand. Although the penalty in Egypt today is not

Faces of Egypt: (facing page) *Fisherman, Hurghada. Watchman, Sakkarah. Bedouin girl, Dahab. Girl and homemade doll, Gurna.*

nearly so severe, the cultural effect remains. An Egyptian will do everything possible to outsmart a tourist in a business deal, but he isn't likely to steal. The crime rate in Cairo is far lower than that in western cities; violent crime is extremely rare.

Egyptian society is very class conscious, and upward mobility is difficult for the lower classes. In the cities they do the menial work that no one else wants to do; in Upper Egypt and the Nile Delta they work the land. The middle class consists of white collar workers, many employed by the government. English is the nation's second language — after Arabic — due largely to the heritage of British colonialism. Upper class families often send their children abroad to study; it is not unusual for them to speak German, French and English in addition to their native tongue.

The role of women in the Middle East may disturb feminists. The man is the boss, and the woman's duty is to serve him. Women of marital age are expected to dress modestly, making no attempt to look attractive to anyone but their husbands. Educated Egyptian women in the cities tend to wear western clothes, but the current trend is toward more conservative dress. In the rural areas and small towns,

The classic beauty of the Ibn Tulun Mosque dates back to 800 AD.

RAMADAN

In Islam, the prophet Mohammed commanded his people to observe the month of Ramadan as a manifestation of their faith. From dawn to sunset they are forbidden to eat, drink, smoke, have sex, or indulge in evil thoughts. It is a difficult time for Muslims and visitors alike, especially if it occurs during the heat of the summer.

Although business is conducted on the western calendar, Muslims reckon time on the lunar calendar for religious purposes. Therefore Ramadan, the ninth month, begins eleven days earlier each year. It is a time of joy and festivity as well as sacrifice. Even when it occurs in summer, Muslims will drink no water and eat no food during the daylight hours. But as soon as the sun sets they sit down to a huge meal. Special dishes are prepared during Ramadan that are not eaten at other times of the year. In the old days, families would celebrate by playing games and telling stories during the evening. Today there is a special television show each night with singing, dancing and comedy.

People celebrate, and the devout ones pray, well into the night. They sleep a few hours, then awake before dawn to eat another large meal before the sun rises.

Needless to say, productivity suffers during this time. The people are weak from fasting, lack of sleep, and dehydration. Absenteeism from work is much higher than normal; most stores and offices close at 2 PM. If you really need to get something done in Egypt, Ramadan is the wrong time to attempt it.

Travelers and people who are sick are exempted from fasting. And, of course, it is not expected of tourists. Most Red Sea dive guides don't observe the Ramadan fast because of the travel exemption, so business goes on as usual in the diving areas.

they wear the traditional black, with their heads covered.

Egyptians tend to look upon western women as easy, especially when dressed in shorts or low-cut dresses. This is the reason for the stares and comments on the streets. The men are not likely to approach, however, unless the woman appears to invite it. In the Red Sea diving areas dress isn't a problem; standard resort wear is the norm.

Hospitality is a strong element of Egyptian culture and religion. To refuse hospitality is considered an insult. This can be awkward when your host picks up the tab for a big meal and you know you can afford it more easily than he can. Just bear it and be gracious, and make him promise to let you pay next time.

Egyptians are a warm, open, demonstrative people. Almost every conversation is passionate. Watching and listening, you may think they are about to come to blows; but arguments are usually resolved amicably. They do a lot of hugging, touching and kissing. When men meet, they often embrace and kiss each other on the cheek. A handshake begins with a hearty slap of hands and often continues through the first part of the conversation.

Getting along with Egyptians is easy as long as you remember that you are a guest in their country. Be open to their opinions, their traditions, and their way of life. You will come away from Egypt with a lot more than a diving vacation. You will learn about a fascinating country, and can make lifelong friends.

CLIMATE AND SEASONS

The high season for tourism in Egypt is during the northern winter, from November through April. During these months, hotel rates are higher and accommodations harder to schedule. It is also the time of heavy diver pressure even though the water is colder, visibility not quite so good, and wind and sea conditions less favorable than during the summer months.

For wealthy Europeans, wintering in Egypt used to be the thing to do, both culturally and socially. But today, with air conditioning in most hotels, summer travel is an attractive alternative. There is always a cool haven to retreat to after a hard day's touring or diving.

The Bedouins are a proud people swearing allegiance to no country. Many still maintain their nomadic way of life. (photo by Mia Tegner)

Since nearly the entire country is a desert, the summer heat is dry and it usually cools off pleasantly at night.

On the Red Sea, the prevailing winds combine with low humidity to make summer temperatures seem considerably cooler than they really are. Although it is in the 100s nearly every day, it feels more like 85. Only when the wind is calm does one become aware of the heat. This can become a problem in terms of sunburn and heat injuries. The desert sun is quite intense, especially when reflected off the surface of the sea. A cap or visor and sunglasses are necessities. Ration your time in the sun, and protect your skin with sunscreens as well as shirts. It would be a shame to miss diving time because of sunburn.

IBM, OR UNDERSTANDING EGYPTIANS

This heading has nothing to do with the big conglomerate that makes computers. It stands for three Arabic words: Inshallah, Bukra and Malesh. An understanding of them and their significance can help a tourist relax and enjoy his trip to Egypt.

Inshallah means "God willing," as in "The dive boat will leave at 8:30 sharp, Inshallah." No appointments or plans are made in Egypt without that escape clause. If the event doesn't come off on time, or not at all, it's because Allah didn't will it. After a couple of your best laid plans are subjected to last minute changes, you will understand the term's significance. Many of the things we take for granted are still minor miracles in Egypt. That includes telephone calls, rapid transportation, and even running water or electricity. Any one of them is subject to sudden shutdown, which could have an impact on schedules and plans. It's a hard life, and in order to accept it stoically, you have to understand the principle of "Inshallah."

Bukra means "tomorrow." It just means the pace of life is slower, and if something doesn't happen today, it will happen tomorrow, or tomorrow, or... After all, in a country with 5,000 years of history, what is one day? If your itinerary called for Abu Nuhas today and the wind from the north is churning the sea into whitecaps, perhaps you can make it Bukra. There are lots of good dive sites to the south. And if you run out of Bukras, the only word left is Malesh.

Malesh is a complex concept. It means a lot of things, including "OK,"or "It doesn't matter," or "There's nothing you can do about it, so why worry?" It explains how the Egyptian accepts his lot in life with a minimum of complaint and without envy of those more fortunate. Perhaps productivity suffers. To be sure, many of Egypt's leaders deplore the "malesh mentality" and maintain that the country will never achieve greatness as long as it persists. But given the problems of everyday existence, perhaps this is a way to cope without becoming dejected or mean. Who is to say that our way is better?

CLOTHES FOR EGYPT by Mia Tegner

Despite the climate, Egyptian dress doesn't resemble westerners' garb for hot weather. Part of the reason might be due to their adaptation, except the locals often look and act as uncomfortable as visitors when it's really hot. Islamic culture expects modest dress, especially for women, and long robes are the traditional garb of desert dwellers. While some Cairo women's styles would fit in on the streets of fashionable American or European cities, many women wear dresses with high necks and long sleeves. For the very religious, scarves are pinned to hide all of their hair and full length skirts cover their legs. In the villages, long black dresses and head scarves are the norm for women, and most of the men wear long robes called gala-biyahs. Egyptian families flock to the beaches in the summer, the men in swimsuits and the women fully dressed. Confined to such get-ups, it was not surprising that few Egyptian women enter the water.

Western women certainly aren't expected to dress like their Egyptian counterparts, but they are likely to feel more comfortable in clothes that don't attract attention. Like dive resorts everywhere, the uniform along the Red Sea seems to be shorts and T shirts over bathing suits by day and a summer dress for dinner. However, once away from the water, the atmosphere changes. In Cairo, I felt most comfortable during the day in a lightweight dress, or skirt and blouse, with sandals. I don't wear long sleeves and high necks, but I do leave low cut or spaghetti strap styles at home. Things are less formal in Upper Egypt, although people generally dress up a bit for dinner at hotels and on cruise ships. For touring the temples and tombs, I recommend a pair of cotton culottes or conservative shorts. The best way to see any country is to do a lot of walking; comfortable footwear is essential when climbing monuments in 115 degree heat. We found small daypacks useful for carrying water bottles, guide books, camera gear, etc., on sightseeing and boat trips. To beat the heat of Upper Egypt, remember that woven fabrics breathe better than knits and that cotton is far superior to synthetics. In addition to the heat, Egypt is dusty; clothes get dirty a lot faster than you might have thought possible. This puts a high priority on items that can be easily rinsed out and hung up to dry. Even in the summer, bring a sweater or light jacket. You aren't likely to need it outside but some facilities, especially the Nile cruise boats, are overly enthusiastic with their air conditioning.

When packing for your dive trip, no matter what time of the year you are going, include a windbreaker and/or sweatshirt. The ever present winds can be quite cool around the water. Additional warm clothes are in order if you go during any season other than summer, especially if you are camping. Despite the coral reefs, Egypt is in the temperate zone. A hat and some sort of coverup are essential protection from the sun. If you have the opportunity before your dive trip, a traditional cotton galabiyah works well. If you plan to climb Mount Sinai, blue jeans, a jacket and running shoes will make the trip more comfortable.

RED SEA WEATHER

June through October are the warm water months in the Red Sea. Water temperatures range from 76 to 82 degrees on the surface. This is not an area conducive to diving without a protective suit; unless

A titan triggerfish, Balistoides viridescens, *aggressively defends its nest against an intruding diver.*

BEATING THE HEAT

Summer is the off season in Egypt. Prices are lower and accommodations less crowded. But even on the Red Sea, where you might not be aware of the temperature due to the low humidity and the prevailing wind, heat will have its effect. If you aren't careful, heat cramps, heat exhaustion, or heat stroke could result.

Heat injuries are easier to prevent than to cure. First of all, acclimatize. Give your body a chance to get used to the heat before carrying on strenuous activity. Most people can make the adjustment in about a week. Try to avoid physical activity in the hottest part of the day. Many Egyptian businesses close from noon to four, then reopen in the evening and at night. Take a cue from the natives. Stay in the shade whenever possible. It doesn't take long to get that Red Sea tan.

Diving dehydrates you through breathing dry air and immersion dialysis (stimulation of kidney function by the chemical effect of salt water). You lose a lot of moisture through perspiration, although you won't be aware of it because sweat evaporates immediately in a dry climate. Therefore, fluid intake is essential. Drink lots of water, fruit juices, or soft drinks. Beer doesn't help, because alcohol is a dehydrating agent. Carry a water bottle in your pack, take frequent drinks, and slow down the pace. If you feel thirsty, your body is trying to tell you something.

Along with fluid, your body loses essential salts while sweating. All warnings about excessive salt intake should be placed on hold in a hot climate. Add more salt to your food; your body needs it to maintain chemical balance and to retain water. Salt tablets are not a good method; they could cause nausea. It's best just to use the salt shaker more heavily at mealtime.

Ignoring these precautions could result in one of three heat injuries. In heat cramps, the loss of essential salts —

BEATING THE HEAT (*continued*)

especially potassium — can cause painful muscle spasms. The treatment is massage, rest, and replacement of fluids and salt. A more serious problem is heat exhaustion. The victim becomes weak and nauseous, and might faint. The skin is cold and clammy, the heartbeat fast but weak. The face will be pale. To treat for heat exhaustion, lay the victim down in the shade with the feet elevated. If he or she is conscious, give liquids, preferably water. A teaspoon of salt and baking soda per quart of water is helpful. Recovery is usually rapid.

If the symptoms are ignored, heat stroke — a life-threatening emergency — may result. In this case, the victim's temperature regulatory mechanism stops functioning, leading to high fever. The face will be red, hot, and dry to the touch. The heartbeat will be rapid and strong. The victim may be unconscious or delirious. If not properly treated, permanent brain damage or death may result. Get the victim out of the sun, elevate the head and shoulders slightly, and do everything possible to cool him down. Sponge baths, wet garments, or even immersion in water will help until medical attention arrives. See that the victim gets to a doctor as quickly as possible.

Remember, heat injuries are much easier to prevent than to cure. Following the procedures outlined here will help you enjoy your Red Sea trip without mishaps.

you are quite active underwater, you will tend to get chilled. Thermoclines are sometimes encountered, but an eighth-inch (3 mm) wetsuit is sufficient. A full suit is recommended for protection from stinging creatures as well as for warmth. On slow-moving night dives, an eighth-inch vest will provide additional warmth.

After diving, the warm wind acts like a blow dryer to quickly evaporate the water off your body and warm you up. If you get chilled on a sedentary photo dive, warmth and comfort will return quickly when you remove your wetsuit. Leaving it on will keep you cold longer due to evaporation.

Dive guides, perhaps spoiled by the warm water, tend to wear quarter- inch (7mm) suits year round. More likely, they need them because of the waiting they have to do for visiting underwater photographers.

During the winter months a quarter-inch farmer john suit is recommended for everyone. Water temperatures range from 70 to 76 degrees. On the surface, air temperatures will be in the 70s but the strong wind chill factor will make it seem colder. A sweater or a medium weight jacket is necessary on the boat between dives, especially at night.

Visibility is generally better during the summer months, averaging 100 feet. In the winter it is about 20 feet less, although 150 feet plus is possible at any time. Plankton blooms — usually occurring in February, March and April — can drop visibility to 15 feet. They are localized and unpredictable, sometimes there in the morning and gone in the afternoon. Tidal currents have a strong effect on visibility.

The prevailing winds (called Shamal) are from the north and northwest, all year round. Generally it is windier in the winter; occasional southern squalls blow at that time. Even in summer there are fewer than ten calm days a month on average. The normal pattern is for the winds to blow in the morning, calm down in the afternoon, then begin again late at night. Whitecaps are almost an everyday occurence, but that doesn't stop the boats from going out. Rides can be bouncy and wet when going uphill in all but the largest vessels. On the other hand, big swells are rare except in the far south. The calmest sea conditions usually occur in August and September; that is the best time to attempt a run to the remote islands of the central Red Sea.

Fish seem to be less active in the winter months, and soft corals appear to shrink and contract. Fewer groupers are seen; they are thought to head for deeper water. On the other hand, January and February is mating season for manta rays. They can always be seen during that time at certain sites, like Shab El Erg. December through February is mating time for sharks, especially around Shadwan Island. They are often agressive toward each other at that time, probably part of the courting ritual.

The new hotels built in the late 1980s offer a new standard of luxury and convenience for Red Sea diving enthusiasts.

DIVING ACCOMMODATIONS

As is the case anywhere else, your comfort level will be almost directly proportional to the price you pay. The high end of the scale is represented by the live-aboard cruise boats. Most of them run out of Sharm el Sheikh, some out of Eilat, Israel. They dive primarily the Sinai region, concentrating on Ras Muhammed and the Straits of Tiran, but many continue on to the reefs of the Hurghada area. (See sidebar: Live- aboard Boats, Chapter V.)

It pays to shop around, but make sure you are comparing the same travel packages. The higher priced operations usually offer more personalized service, with guides who take care of your every need on land and on the water. If you are leery about your first trip to the Middle East, this could be the way to go. The experienced traveler might want to save money and do more for him or herself.

Land-based operations in Sinai have experienced a building boom, with three new privately-owned hotels and dive centers opening in 1987. These are in addition to the existing facilities which date

AVERAGE TEMPERATURES

Listed in the chart below are the average air temperatures for Cairo and for Hurghada throughout the year. The Red Sea has a moderating influence on the hot desert air, so temperatures near the water are usually quite pleasant. Temperatures at Sharm El Sheikh were not available, but they are similar to Hurghada. Upper Egypt (the southern part of the country) is considerably hotter than Cairo. Temperatures may hit 120 degrees farenheit in summer.

Month	Cairo		Hurghada	
	Low	High	Low	High
January	47	66	49	69
February	49	69	49	70
March	52	75	54	73
April	57	82	61	79
May	63	90	69	85
June	64	94	74	88
July	70	95	77	91
August	71	95	77	91
September	68	90	74	87
October	65	86	67	83
November	62	75	60	78
December	51	69	53	72

back to the Israeli period. The new hotels feature such amenities as swimming pools, restaurants, snack bars, and even a disco. Full-course meals are a part of most hotel packages. They will also pack box lunches for day trips if notified in advance.

The new dive centers are larger, more efficiently laid out, and even have air-conditioned classrooms. Competition from the new operations will also result in upgrading of services and facilities in the existing ones if they are to survive. Old-time travelers to the area will probably suffer future shock as Naama Bay facilities have taken a 20-year jump into the future.

Sinai dive centers rent tanks, weight belts, regulators, buoyancy compensators and wetsuits, although it is best to bring as much of your own equipment as possible. Guided dive trips are run on daily schedules, some from the beach and some from boats. More dive boats are being brought into the area, both for day trips and live-aboards, but during the high season boat trips may still not be available every day. Transportation to beach diving sites is by truck or van. There is no surf, and entries usually consist of walking less than 50 yards of shallow coral reef, then stepping off the edge. (Be sure to bring a sturdy set of booties for those walks.)

Water is piped in from inland wells, and a desalinization plant went on line in 1987. But this is a desert, fresh water is precious, and occasionally the system breaks down. This can be frustrating when your body and equipment is salty, but service is usually restored within a day.

Electricity is 220 volts, 50 cycles, and uses European sockets. Bring along a voltage converter for charging lights and strobes. Remember, it will take about 20 percent longer to charge batteries that are designed for 60 cycles. Current is normally on 24 hours a day, but failures are not unheard of.

Hurghada is a larger city with a greater range of tourist facilities. Its building boom preceded Naama Bay's by a year or two. Hotels at the low end of the price range are geared toward the European market, with dormitory type accomodations and no air conditioning, but are generally clean. Two to six persons sleep in a room, with a ceiling fan, sharing a common bathroom.

The high end establishments are rated four stars, making allow-ance for the location. Rooms are air conditioned and clean, and res-taurants specialize in impressive buffets, with a bar and entertain-ment at night. Water is rationed in Hurghada; even the expensive hotels shut off the taps during daytime hours.

Large tourist villages are almost self-contained towns with full dining and recreation programs included in the price. Diving may be included, but it is also possible to stay at one of these locations and dive with an operator in town.

Separate dive packages may be arranged through the Hurghada centers. Nearly all consist of boat trips; there are few beach diving sites in the area. Most dive centers have their own boats, based on expanded versions of the rugged wooden fishing boats. Live-aboards are also available from Hurghada, although not as many as in Sinai.

A school of masked butterfly fish greet a diver at Ota Abu Rimata.

Chapter 3

The Red Sea: A Scientific View

by Mia J. Tegner, Ph.D.
Scripps Institution of Oceanography

A ny discussion of man's history in the Red Sea, or the spectacular marine life beneath its surface, requires an understanding of the physical forces which shape this region. Just as various geographic and ecological factors have acted to make the Red Sea flora and fauna different from other areas of the world ocean, physical factors have affected man's use of this waterway. Although a newcomer compared to the marine life, man has traveled on the Red Sea for a long time; this is one of the first large bodies of water mentioned in recorded history. Yet conditions are so harsh that few people live there, even today.

The Geological Setting

Anyone studying a map of northeast Africa and the Arabian Peninsula will be struck by the apparent jigsaw fit that appears possible by closing the Red Sea. The Red Sea occupies a large and slowly growing rift valley between the continents of Africa and Asia. Part of the world rift system, the Red Sea is a segment of the African Rift which extends though Tanzania, Kenya and Ethiopia, up the sea itself, then northward through the Gulf of Aqaba and into the Dead Sea. Beyond the Gulf of Aden, this rift joins the Carlsberg Rift in the Indian Ocean and the world oceanic rift system.

Geologically speaking, the Red Sea is very young, roughly 40 million years old. Before that time, Africa and the Arabian Peninsula were both part of the primeval megacontinent of Gondwanaland. The evolution of the Red Sea probably began about 42 million years ago with a rift propagating westward from the Arabian Sea into the Afro-Arabian landmass, leading to the formation of the Gulf of Aden. The crack spread through the western Gulf of Aden, then progressively up the Red Sea. During the second stage of the development, which began 24 to 25 million years ago, sea floor spreading led to considerable widening of the Gulf of Aden and the Red Sea. In the north, a new rift propagated north-northeast creating the Gulf of Aqaba and the Dead Sea. Arabia moved 62 kilometers to the north of Sinai, opening the northern Red Sea.

62

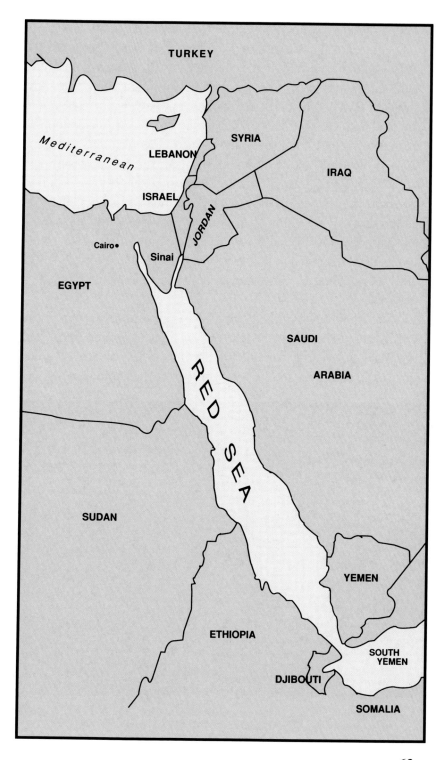

TURKEY

Mediterranean

LEBANON

SYRIA

IRAQ

ISRAEL

JORDAN

Cairo•

Sinai

EGYPT

SAUDI

ARABIA

RED SEA

SUDAN

YEMEN

ETHIOPIA

SOUTH
YEMEN

DJIBOUTI

SOMALIA

This rotation of Arabia closed the Red Sea in the south and led to extensive deposits of evaporites (sedimentary rocks formed by the evaporation of seawater in the enclosed basin). After a tectonically quiet period, a new rift began about five million years ago. The straits of Bab-el-Mandeb were opened, allowing water to flow into the Red Sea from the Indian Ocean and ending the deposition of evaporites. Sea floor spreading formed a deep trough along the axis of the Red Sea as the evaporite layer broke apart and new oceanic crust was formed. As the sea opened, a further 45 kilometer shear occured along the Aqaba-Dead Sea Rift. The pattern of earthquakes, the alignment of active volcanoes along the trough axis, and the flow of hot brines from the depths of the axial trough in recent times indicate that the Red Sea is still evolving. Arabia and Africa continue to move apart at the pace of about half an inch per year.

The importance of the geology for our purposes is what it can tell us about the origin of the marine life in the Red Sea. The original waters came from the Mediterranean Sea (an arm of which once extended as far south as Qeseir) before the geological activity

Carvings from the funerary temple of Queen Hatshepsut accurately depict Red Sea fishes, showing that the ancients were familiar with these creatures.

described above. This connection with the Mediterranean Sea fluctuated with the repeated emergence and submergence of the Isthmus of Suez. The sea eventually opened to the Indian Ocean in the south. Fossil remains along the Red Sea coasts show successive layers of mixed Mediterranean and Indo-Pacific fossils alternating with layers of almost pure Indo-Pacific origin. During the ice ages, when sea levels dropped worldwide, some scientists believe that the Red Sea was isolated from other bodies of water and that excessive evaporation led to such high salinity that little life survived. Thus, the present-day forms date to the reopening of the Straits of Bab-el-Mandeb to the Indian Ocean.

Today, the Red Sea is a long, narrow basin, about 2,000 kilometers in length and averaging 280 kilometers in width. The average depth is 491 meters, but the deep axial troughs reach 2,500 meters. The Straits of Bab-el-Mandeb in the south are 26 kilometers wide and only about 100 meters deep, sharply limiting the exchange of water with the Indian Ocean. In the northeast, the Red Sea ends in the Gulf of Aqaba, a narrow, deep (maximum depth over 1800 meters) trough which has no connection to another body of water.

METRIC CONVERSION

Most countries, as well as science, utilize the metric system of weights and measures. Because this book utilizes both the metric and English systems, conversion factors are presented here.

MEASURE

0.39 inches	1 centimeter
1 inch	2.54 centimeters
1 foot	30 meters
39.37 inches	1 meter
0.62 miles	1 kilometer
1 mile	1.61 kilometers

WEIGHT

0.04 ounces	1 gram
1 ounce	28.35 grams
1 pound	453.59 grams
2.2 pounds	kilogram
1 ton	907.18 kilograms

TEMPERATURE

Farenheit to Celsius: Subtract 32 from Farenheit temperature, multiply by 5, then divide by 9. Celsius to Farenheit: Multiply Celsius temperature by 9, then divide by 5, then add 32.

Climate

Surrounded by deserts, the Red Sea is located in a hot, arid region. The northern Red Sea is dominated by persistent northwest winds throughout the year. The rest of the Sea and the Gulf of Aden are subject to the influence of the Indian monsoons (seasonally reversing winds that affect much of Asia). The northern Red Sea is relatively cool, but the region south of 18 degrees North and the shores of the Gulf of Aden are considered to be among the hottest areas in the world. Rainfall is extremely low. While occasional frontal systems from the Mediterranean Sea strike the north in the winter (cloudbursts in the mountains of the Sinai led to floods at Naama Bay and Dahab in recent years), the average annual rainfall at Suez is 21 millimeters (less than an inch) and only 3 millimeters at Hurghada. Although rainfall is somewhat higher in other areas of the Red Sea, only one river, the Baraka in Sudan, flows into the Sea.

Oceanography

The Red Sea's geology and climate are important determinants of its oceanography. The semi-enclosed basin, the strong winds and arid climate which cause evaporation to be much greater than precipitation, and the minimal freshwater input from rivers all act to make the Red Sea the saltiest body of water still attached to the world ocean. The average net evaporation is more than two meters of seawater per year. To compensate for this evaporation, inflow through the Straits of Bab-el-Mandeb is greater than outflow throughout the year. But the Straits are narrow and shallow relative to the size of the Sea, restricting mixing with waters of the Indian Ocean. As a result, salinity and temperature are higher and dissolved oxygen and nutrients are lower than in other seas. Surface water salinity increases from south (the region of inflow from the Straits) to the north, due to evaporation and mixing with more saline deep water. The salinity in the northern Red Sea is about 40 parts per thousand, whereas average salinities in open ocean waters are generally 33 to 35 parts per thousand.

These factors govern circulation as well as water properties. In the winter, surface water flows north, grows denser because of evaporation and cooling, eventually sinking in the northern Red Sea. This water then returns south as high salinity subsurface water that flows out over the sill at Bab-el-Mandeb. The surface current flows north in the winter against the prevailing winds to compensate for the water which sinks. In the summer, reversal of the monsoon winds leads to a reversal of the surface current in the southern Red Sea. Surface water flows south causing upwelling in the northern Red Sea. Warm, high salinity water flows out of the Straits over a subsurface inflow of cooler, less salty water.

Red Sea tides are also affected by geology. Movements of the

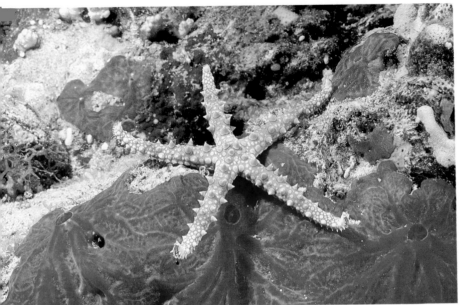

This sea star, Gomophia aegyptiaca, *is one of the Red Sea's many colorful species*

earth and moon relative to the sun set up a simple oscillation of the waters in the long, narrow basin. There is a six-hour lag between the time of high water in the north and south. The average spring tidal range is about 0.5 meters at the two ends of the Sea and decreases towards the center where there is no appreciable semi-diurnal rhythm. The tides get larger approaching the northern ends of both the Gulf of Suez and the Gulf of Aqaba, where the range is more than 1.0 meter. In addition to the tides, there is a seasonal variation in mean sea level with a general decrease in summer influenced by the monsoons. Sea level also decreases about 30 centimeters from the south to the north year round.

Because of the intense solar radiation in this part of the world and the minimal mixing with the rest of the world ocean, surface water temperatures are relatively high for these latitudes. Because of the shallow sill at Bab-el-Mandeb and the geothermal activity in the deep axial troughs, subsurface temperatures are considerably warmer. At a depth of 1,000 meters, the Red Sea is about 21 degrees C, whereas Indian Ocean water is about 6-8 degrees C at the same depth. In the hot, saline deeps, temperatures reach 56 degrees C and the salinity is over 250 parts per thousand. Geologists have estimated that heavy metal deposits in the Red Sea deeps are worth hundreds of millions of dollars because of the concentrations of copper, zinc, silver, gold, iron and manganese. These metals could be mined from either the muddy oozes under the deeps or the hot, saline water itself. Recent studies suggest that if mine tailings are disposed of into deep water (below 1,000 meters), these metals could be mined with minimal environmental impact to marine life.

Biological Oceanography

Just as geology and climate shape the oceanogaphy of the Red Sea, all these factors affect the biological processes and communities that are found beneath its surface. In other areas of the world, rivers carry nutrients to the sea which support open-water plant growth or primary productivity and fisheries. Virtually without river input, the surface waters of the Red Sea are low in nutrients, so open-water stocks of phytoplankton (single-celled algae at the base of the food chain) and zooplankton (tiny, free-swimming

Two clownfish, Amphiprion bicinctus, *seek shelter within the tentacles of a symbiotic anemone. This species is found only in the Red Sea.*

69

animals) are low. The low phytoplankton concentration is comparable with other unproductive areas of the world ocean such as the Sargasso Sea. Not surprisingly, the area does not support much in the way of open-water fisheries. However, as we will discuss later, plankton abundance is very different over coral reefs.

The same conditions which are bad for open-water productivity promote coral growth. Reef-building corals require warm, clear waters and have minimal tolerance for sedimentation or influxes of fresh water. Corals cannot survive winter temperatures below 18 degrees C and the boundary to their worldwide distribution is set by this temperature. The desert climate maintains water temperatures well above normal for these latitudes, and the reefs at the north end of the Red Sea are among the most northerly fully developed reefs in the world. Reef-building corals require considerable light; because of the low primary productivity and lack of sediment, light penetrates to great depths in the clear water. Sediments, often borne by rivers, clog coral mouths and tentacles, interfering with their breathing and feeding. Too much dilution of

Table corals are found along many of Sinai's walls. This formation is at Paradise.

seawater can kill the animals. Clearly, coral reefs and large rivers don't mix.

Large storms, hurricanes or typhoons, are a major source of coral mortality in other parts of the world. A regular feature of the Caribbean and South Pacific, such storms are not known in the Red Sea. However, one weather-associated mass mortality of corals has been documented in Eilat, at the northern end of the Gulf of Aqaba. Atmospheric conditions apparently caused an abnormal depression of sea level and coral colonies on the reef table were exposed to air longer than the normal tidal cycle. In this case, the massive brain-like corals were much more resistant to the harmful effects of dry air than the more delicate bush-like forms.

The importance of geology to marine life is the restriction of inflow from the Gulf of Aden and the Indian Ocean by the Straits of Bab-el-Mandeb. The Red Sea is the northwesternmost extension of a vast, continuous stretch of the tropical ocean which includes the Indian and Pacific Oceans. Biologists, who use geographic barriers and thermal gradients to divide the ocean into provinces with characteristic groups of organisms, call this region the Indo-Pacific. While few organisms range throughout this huge area, many are found over thousands of kilometers. The marine life of the Red Sea is almost completely Indo-Pacific in origin, but some differences are apparent. These differences can be traced to the effects of the narrow straits. Restricted water flow with the Indian Ocean reduces exchange of larvae (the dispersal phase of most animals) and is important in creating and mantaining the more extreme temperature and salinity conditions in the Red Sea.

As a result of adaptation to Red Sea conditions, a number of species are now endemic (unique) to this area. It has been esti-mated that 10 percent of all the fish species found in the Red Sea are endemic and about 90 percent are found over broad areas of the Indo-Pacific. The lack of variation between fishes of this latter group caught in and outside of the Red Sea indicates that they are not isolated from each other. However, the proportion of endemics varies between different groups of animals, probably in relation to the lengths of their larval phases and their mobility as adults. Over 40 percent of the cowries and 50 percent of the butterfly fishes are

The Napoleon Wrasse, Cheilinus undulatus, *can grow in excess of 400 pounds.*

found only in the Red Sea and the Gulf of Aden. The effects of isolation are especially apparent with deep sea fishes. Because the Straits are shallow and deep-sea physical conditions are very different, there is a scarcity of deep-sea fauna compared to the Indian Ocean.

Overall there are fewer species of many coral reef-associated animal groups in the Red Sea than in the Indo-Pacific province. Some may simply not have been able to adapt as conditions in the Red Sea became saltier and warmer than they were used to. Part of the reason appears to be the distance from the center of the Indo-Pacific. The greatest number of coral species, for example, is found in the center of this region near Indonesia and the Philippines. The number of species drops in all directions from the center and the Red Sea is at the northwestern boundary of the province. However, the reduced number of species will only be apparent to the eyes of a trained specialist. The astonishing variety and abundance of organisms that are in the Red Sea make such arguments somewhat academic.

In recent times (since 1869) the Suez Canal has provided a link

The shallow area at Jackson Reef in the Straits of Tiran is alive with colorful fish and soft corals.

with the Mediterranean Sea, but because it is shallow and narrow, the amount of water exchange is small. The mean higher sea level and greater tidal range in the Gulf of Suez, as compared with Port Said, lead to a weak but detectable current flowing from the Red Sea into the Mediterranean Sea during most of the year. As a result, more fishes have been able to pass from the Red Sea into the Mediterranean, where some have become established and now support fisheries. A few fish species have moved in the opposite direction, but so far none have left the Gulf of Suez. Several factors, including the high temperature of canal waters, and a bottom unfavorable for plant and animal life, have probably worked together to minimize exchange of species between the two seas.

Coral Reef Ecology

Coral reefs are among nature's architectural wonders. Common in clear water throughout the tropics, these communities are remarkable for their great variety of organisms, their profusion of shapes and patterns, and their structural complexity. The rigid framework of coral reefs consists of compacted and cemented calcium carbonate from the skeletons of animals, primarily corals, and from algae, especially encrusting corallines. This limestone foundation is topped by a layer of living organisms, which adds a few millimeters per year to the ancestral reef. Coral polyps may not dominate the biomass of the community, but the existence of other organisms is based on the ability of corals to build a massive, wave-resistant structure. The communal efforts of these small organisms produced the Great Barrier Reef, a 1,950 kilometer-long complex of reefs and islands stretching along much of the east coast of Australia.

Charles Darwin was the first person to make a systematic study of coral reefs and his classification of reef types is still in use today. The three main types are fringing reefs, barrier reefs and atolls, although intermediate forms between these types often confuse the definitions. Fringing reefs, as their name implies, are found along land masses where adequate currents provide the proper temperature and oxygen supplies and there is some sort of firm bottom. Depending on the underlying substrate, fringing reefs can vary widely in size and slope. They lie parallel to the coast and may extend anywhere from 50 meters to over a kilometer from the shore. Often there is a shallow, sandy lagoon between the shoreline and the reef's edge. Because of the arid climate, the fringing reefs of the Red Sea are some of the best developed in the world and are found along virtually all of its shores, except where the rocky coast is interrupted by sandy bays. These bays, called sharms in Arabic, are typically found at the mouths of valleys or washes (called wadis) which carry sediments from rare cloudbursts. Naama Bay is one such sandy bay at the opening of a wash where fringing reefs are not found. Fringing reefs are well developed along the shores of islands. There are extensive islands and coral reef complexes where the Red Sea narrows into the entrances to the Gulfs of Aqaba and Suez.

Barrier reefs are linear structures paralleling the coast some distance (a few kilometers) out to sea. Generally barrier reefs rise from a rock platform or terrace. They are separated from shore by a lagoon. As the lagoon narrows, the barrier reef may become a fringing reef. Along the northern part of the Egyptian coast of the

A typical fringing reef along the Sinai coast drops off into clear, blue water.

Giant sea fans at Ras Nasrani can grow over 20 feet in width.

Red Sea proper, there is an offshore system of hills, some underwater and some forming islands, which supports an interrupted barrier reef.

Atolls are circular reefs rising from very deep water that originated as fringing reefs around islands which have since subsided. There are no atolls in the Egyptian Red Sea.

The Brothers Islands, St. John's Island, and Daedalus Reef are examples of reefs which have developed over sea mounts rising out of very deep water. The limestone cap over black, igneous rock on the Brothers Islands indicates that at some period, either when sea level was higher or the sea mounts were lower, these islands were underwater.

Small sea level reefs which rise from relatively shallow water, such as the continental shelf or the floors of lagoons, are called patch reefs and are often found behind barrier reefs. Their general form is a flat-topped hill, and they range up to perhaps a kilometer in width. There are numerous patch reefs in the Hurghada area including Carless Reef and Shabroor om Gamaar.

This cup coral, family Dendrophyllidae, extends its tentacles at night to feed.

There is a wide variety of different types of corals. The hermatypic or reef building corals (class Scleractinia) are distinguished by production of a skeleton of calcium carbonate, which can develop into massive formations through cumulative growth, and by having symbiotic algae in their tissues. Because corals are attached to the reef, they were thought to be plants well into the eighteenth century. While corals are certainly animals, the presence of zooxanthellae (unicellular algae in their tissues) explains much about the dependence of coral reefs on clear water. The zooxanthellae are involved in the calcification process necessary for corals to grow. The growth rate of hermatypic corals in the light is, on the average, 14 times higher than in the dark. If corals are held in darkness for several weeks, they will release their zooxanthellae. Such corals remain healthy but grow at a very slow rate, even in the light. This symbiotic partnership allows coral polyps measured in millimeters to build reefs kilometers long. The dependence of hermatypic corals on photosynthesis is apparent in their depth distribution. Most grow at depths less than 25 meters and growth rates are highest in waters less than 10 meters. However recent studies, conducted along the Sinai coast with a research submersible, located 47 hermatypic species below 50 meters and 9 species which extended below 100 meters. Their depth distributions are related to good light penetration in the clear waters. Non-reef forming or ahermatypic corals, which feed on plankton, were found as deep as 200 meters. Other reef-inhabiting animals such as sea anemones and some non-reef building coral species also contain zooxanthellae and are therefore more abundant in shallow water.

The Red Sea goldfish, *Anthias sp.*, are found in vast profusion around coral heads and along walls. Corals obtain nutrition from several sources including predation and contributions from the zooxanthellae. Like other members of the coelenterates, the polyps use their nematocyst-bearing tentacles to capture prey. This method of feeding was difficult to explain in view of the well known low density of plankton in tropical waters. In the 1970s scientists discovered a nocturnal zooplankton fauna over reefs which is very different from the zooplankton of surrounding

Large plate corals are adapted to gather maximum light for their symbiotic algae.

oceanic waters. Many varieties of small crustaceans, worms, and other swimming invertebrates hide in holes and crevices within the reef during the day, and emerge into the water column at night. Literally thousands of these creatures emerge from a square meter of coral reef after dark. Corals also use mucus released through their mouths to trap bacteria, phytoplankton and particulate matter. The zooxanthellae, whose role in calcium deposition is so important to coral growth, also fix carbon which ends up in coral tissue as protein and lipids. Photosynthesis appears to be important for the carbon and energy needs of the corals and the capture of zooplankton is important as a nitrogen source.

The wide variety of coral forms might suggest that different species earn their living in different ways and there is good evidence to support this view. Highly carnivorous types which depend primarily on zooplankton capture have large polyps and a low surface area to volume ratio. Corals which depend heavily on their symbiotic algae have branching or plated forms designed for intercepting light, and are characterized by a high surface to volume ratio. Not surprisingly, coral polyps relying heavily on

Schools of Anthias, *the Indo-Pacific "Goldfish" flit around a coral formation like butterflies.*

79

photosynthesis are open during the day, whereas the carnivores are active at night when the zooplankton emerge from the reef.

To the casual observer it is often not apparent that algal productivity on a coral reef is quite high. While productivity is high, little alage is visible because grazing pressure is intense. The different algae types include micoroscopic algae on coral sand, filamentous and encrusting forms which are found boring into or on top of porous reef substrates, and larger algae in and around coral heads. Several biologists have erected cages to exclude grazing sea urchins or fishes from areas of the reef and observed lush growths of filamentous and fleshy algae as a result. These growths disappeared almost immediately when the cages were removed. In contrast to the inconspicuous fleshy algae, encrusting coralline algae or "pink rock" are very obvious on a reef. These algae are more important as reef builders and are a major source of calcium carbonate sediments.

The most important algal grazers in coral reef communities are sea urchins and several groups of fishes including some of the damselfishes (Pomacentridae), surgeonfishes (Acanthuridae), parrotfishes (Scaridae), butterflyfishes (Chaetodontidae), triggerfishes (Balistidae), and rabbitfishes (Siganidae). Parrotfishes and surgeonfishes have strengthened, beak-like teeth for rasping algae encrusted on surfaces or in the reef itself. Because the fishes are somewhat omnivorous or are capable of significant erosion of the substrate, their grazing may damage animals as well. Their rasping activities account for much of the calcareous (sand-like) sediment produced on the reef.

A large number of coral reef animals, both invertebrates and fishes, feed primarily on plankton. Recent work suggests that coral reef zooplankton feed in a different manner than their cold water counterparts which are more dependent on phytoplankton. Corals produce copious amounts of an energy-rich mucus, which collects organic detritus (waste) and is rapidly colonized by bacteria. This mucus is eaten by zooplankton, crabs and fishes. Some animals such as sponges can filter bacteria directly but fragments of this mucus-detritus-bacteria complex may be one of the most important transfers of energy and nutrients in the coral reef ecosystem.

The yellow mark on the mapfish's (Pomacanthus maculosis) *side is supposed to resemble the African continent.*

Examples of zooplankton-feeding fishes are the ubuquitous gold-fish *Anthias squamipinnis,* the blue fusilier, *Caesio lunaris,* silver-sides (Antherinidae), and several species of damselfishes.

Most coral reef fishes are carnivores whether they feed on zooplankton, benthic (living on or near the bottom) invertebrates or other fishes. Many species feed on zooplankton when they are small, and when larger, switch to benthic invertebrates and/or fishes. Wrasses (Labridae) feed on such benthic invertebrates as clams, snails, hermit crabs, sea urchins and brittle stars. Trigger-fishes, which are important as algae eaters, actually are omnivores which eat a wide variety of hard-shelled prey including the living tips of corals. Fish eaters come in a variety of sizes and specialize in different habitats. The small hawkfishes (Cirrhitidae) rest on top of coral heads to feed on crustaceans and small fishes closely associated with living coral. The larger groupers (Serranidae) also sit and wait for crustaceans and reef fishes. Faster moving preda-tors such as the jacks (Carangidae), tunas (Scombridae), and bar-racudas (Sphyraenidae) focus on midwater prey such as schooling fishes.

A school of silver sweepers, Parapriacanthus guentheri, *can sound like a flock of locusts as they swim by the diver's ear.*

To the observer from temperate waters, coral reefs seem to support an overwhelming variety of animal species and the diversity of fishes is especially apparent. To approach the question of why there are so many kinds of fishes, we need to first consider what defines a coral reef fish. Only a small proportion of reef fishes including some of the butterflyfishes, filefishes (Monacanthidae), parrotfishes, triggerfishes and puffers (Tetraondontidae) feed directly on coral polyps. However coral reefs do present surfaces for algae to grow on and habitats for nocturnal zooplankton, two important types of fish food. Similarly, many coral reef fishes are also found on dead coral reefs and seem to do fine without corals and away from the reef. Probably most important, what the coral reef does provide is a fish habitat with a high degree of physical and biological complexity—places to hide from predators. The use of the hiding places varies considerably. Some groups are active by day including damselfishes, wrasses, goatfishes (Mullidae), blennies (Blennidae), butterflyfishes, and surgeonfishes, while others, such as groupers, moray eels (Muraenidae), scorpionfishes (Scorpaenidae), cardinalfishes (Apogonidae), soldierfishes and squirrelfishes (Holocentridae), and flashlight fishes (Anomalopidae) leave their shelters only at dusk.

The diversity of hiding places is reflected in the diversity of fish shapes: long and slender (eels), round (pufferfishes), laterally compressed (butterflyfishes, triggerfishes), and vertically flattened (torpedo rays, flatfishes). The diversity of shapes is augmented by the range of sizes. Some species choose physical holes in the reef, others seek biological shelter. Examples of adaptations to biological habitats include hiding among different species of stony corals, anemone tentacles, the spines of sea urchins, sea grass meadows, and shrimp burrows. Where the diversity of space-shelters is high, there is a large number of fish species present. Areas of relatively uniform coral formations show fewer species but higher abundances. Fishes attracted to the physical structures of the reef for hiding places in turn attract predators, further increasing the diversity of the community. The net result is a fish watcher's delight.

The deadly stonefish, Synanceia verrucosa, *is a master of camouflage. An ambush predator, it often hides in holes within coral heads.*

Chapter 4

Note: An index to Marine life photos appears on pages 110 - 111

CREATURES OF THE RED SEA

F or the diver, the richness and color of the Red Sea's underwater environment is the magnet which brings him here. Descending on a shallow reef or a sheer wall, he is dazzled by the coral formations, and the abundant fish and invertebrate life. Whether captured on film or with the camera of the mind, the images remain vivid long after the traveler returns home.

The more you know about the local reef dwellers, the more you will enjoy your trip to the Red Sea. Marine creatures spend most of their waking hours eating or reproducing, all the while protecting themselves from predators. Many have developed unusual ways to carry on these processes. Some are as obvious as the symbiotic relationship of a clownfish to an anemone, others as subtle as the mimic blenny, a tiny predator — colored like a cleaner wrasse — that nips other fishes waiting to be cleaned. While perhaps not as exciting as facing a shark, observing and understanding life on the reef can be one of the most rewarding aspects of a Red Sea diving vacation.

In this chapter we will examine some of the common reef creatures, focusing on their habits and behavior the way a diver would see them. Included will be tips on how to approach and photograph them. We will also discuss the few potentially dangerous animals and how to encounter them safely.

INVERTEBRATES

CORALS in the Red Sea come in an almost infinite variety of shapes, colors and textures. Corals can be hard or soft, shaped in clumps, plates, branches or fans. All of them sting, but only a few strongly enough that humans can feel it.

On a first visit to the Indo-Pacific, divers are usually overwhelmed by the colors of the SOFT CORALS of the family Nephtheidae. In the Red Sea, these animals are fast growing, opportunistic organisms found in profusion in many areas, especially where there are currents. The translucent branches, in brilliant reds, purples, pinks and oranges, are partially supported by hard calcium spicules. The bodies transmit light, so top and backlighting is often effective in photographs. They are such easy, beautiful subjects that merciless editing is necessary to avoid an entire slide show of nothing but soft corals.

One type of soft coral with small, feathery tentacles on white stems, grows in low-lying colonies. They look like hundreds of mouths, alternately opening and closing. An encounter with *Xenia* is one event that video can capture better than a still photograph.

Large BLACK CORAL trees, Antipathes, are usually found in deeper waters because the shallow ones have long since been collected. But in the Red Sea, "deeper" means 60 to 100 feet. What little harvesting that was done had been stopped before all the animals were taken from diving depths. In remote places like The Brothers, black corals are found as shallow as 20 feet. These colonies grow extremely slowly, so the larger ones are very old. Their feathery branches look brown underwater.

SEA FANS are another type of colonial coelenterate closely related to corals. In the Red Sea, some gorgonian species grow to spans of 20 feet. Since they are dependent upon water-borne nutrients, most of the larger ones are located on walls or points exposed to

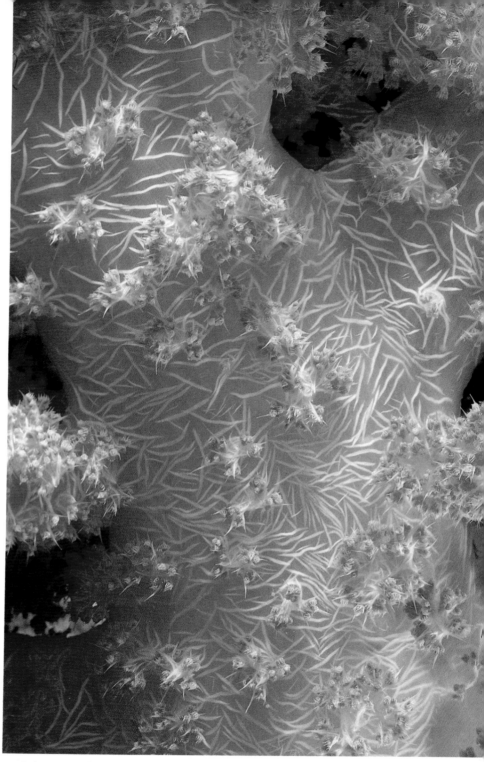

Calcium spicules help to support the body of soft corals.

Fromia *sp. is a common sea star in this area.*

strong currents. When photographing them, try to include a diver for a sense of scale. The Red Sea is not a great area for SPONGES. Many species are there, but they lack the brilliant colors and the large size of those found in the Caribbean. Many are encrusting sponges, which appear as patches of color on the reef, especially on the undersides of coral formations and cave ceilings.

Most SEA STARS are small and inconspicuous. An especially beautiful but tiny one, *Fromia* sp., has a red and white pattern, reminding one of a candy cane. The largest, *Acanthaster*, the CROWN OF THORNS Starfish, feeds on corals. However, it has not made a significant impact on Red Sea reefs. Avoid touching *Acanthaster's* spines, because people with sensitivity can develop severe reactions to the mucus they produce.

At night, BASKET STARS dominate the shallow areas of the reefs, their arms spread in the current to trap small organisms. Members of the brittle star family, some grow to have armspans as long as a person. They don't like divers' lights and begin to retract their arms when illuminated.

CRINOIDS, or feather stars, are another nocturnal echinoderm.

The Crown of Thorns, Acanthaster, *eats coral, but has not been a problem in the Egyptian Red Sea. Be careful of its toxic spines.*

Red Sea varieties come in many colors, including a range of soft pastels. They perch on the coral with a row of tiny feet called cirri. Lift them gently with a finger under the feet and they will "fly," slowly waving their feathery arms. Don't grab the arms, because they are extremely brittle and will break off. With extension tubes and backlighting, dramatic photographs can be made of the arms and the tiny hairs on the "feathers."

A wide variety of MOLLUSCS are found in the waters of the Red Sea. Most of them are cryptic or nocturnal. It is forbidden to take any live coral or shell, so the diver's interest in these creatures should be limited to observation and photography.

The *Tridacna,* or GIANT CLAM, isn't a giant in the Red Sea. Most are under a foot across; they do not attain the massive size of those in the South Pacific. They are generally found in shallow water because the commensal algae living in the mantle need sunlight for photosynthesis. These algae lend beautiful turquoise and emerald patterns to the mantle. Sensitive to movement and shadow, the mantle might initially retract when you move in for a photograph. Just be patient and it will return. A good time to photograph them is

The giant clam, Tridacna, *is usually found in shallow water, where sunlight is utilized by the algae living in its mantle.*

at dusk when they are less sensitive to movement.

Several species of NUDIBRANCHS are common, but finding them requires close observation. The largest is the nocturnal SPAN-ISH DANCER, *Hexabranchus sanguineus*, which can exceed a foot in length. When picked up from the reef at night and tossed upward, this animal swims by undulating its entire body. The white stripe around the perimeter of its bright red mantle makes it look like the skirts of a Flamenco dancer. Often the performance continues until the diver carefully replaces the nudibranch into a crevice within the reef.

The most common of the smaller nudibranchs is *Chromidoris quadricolor*, or the PAJAMA NUDIBRANCH. Its body markings of white, yellow, black and orange resemble striped pajamas. Nudibranchs eat sponges and hydroids, and have the ability to incorporate the nematocysts (stinging cells) into their own body for protection. If a fish ingests one, it quickly gets stung and spits it out. Other nudibranchs have chemicals in their body that taste so bad, the fishes learn to leave them alone. Most Red Sea nudibranchs are small enough to require extension tubes to photograph them, gener-

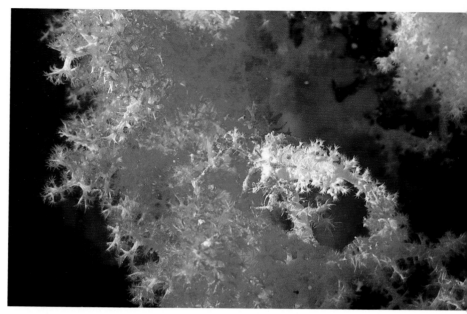

A tiny decorator crab attaches bits of soft coral to its body, rendering it almost invisible against its colorful background.

ally of a 1:2 or greater reproduction ratio.

OCTOPUSES are usually cryptic, preferring to hide in holes during the day. Look for accumulations of shells around the entrance to the lair. Finding one in the open is strictly a matter of chance, and chances are better at night. CUTTLEFISH are also active after sunset and the chances of seeing one on a night dive are good. A relative of squids and octopuses, this cephalopod looks like a small fish at first glance because its tentacles are short and not very obvious. The cuttlefish is a master of camouflage and can change color almost instantly.

Most CRUSTACEANS in the Red Sea are nocturnal. Three species of SPINY LOBSTERS are found there, all members of the family Palinuridae. At night they roam the shallowest part of the reef. Fishermen often hunt them at night, walking through the ankle deep water of the reeftop with flashlights. Slipper lobsters generally prefer deeper water.

On a night dive, several varieties of CRABS are likely to be encountered. They range in size from the tiny white spider crab to larger ones about the size of a fist. One of the most interesting is the

DECORATOR CRAB, which camouflages itself by attaching bits of living matter to its carapace. Only when seeing a group of tiny sponges and soft corals moving about the reef do you realize the true nature of this assemblage.

During the day, HERMIT CRABS actively roam the reef seeking food. They take over empty shells to protect their soft carapace. The key to photographing a hermit crab is patience. When disturbed, it will retract into the shell for several minutes, but eventually it will come back out. When that happens, the creature will usually submit to several strobe pictures.

FISHES

It would take a volume many times this size to cover even a small percentage of the more than 1,000 species of fishes in the Red Sea. Instead, we will examine the major families of fishes, and discuss a few from each that a diver is likely to encounter. Sharks, rays, lionfish, morays and scorpionfish are covered in the section on potentially dangerous creatures at the end of this chapter.

LIZARDFISH (Syndontidae) are common throughout the world's tropical seas. These bottom-dwelling fishes, about six to eight inches long, have a face which resembles a lizard's, along with sharp teeth. They lie on sand bottoms, and ambush prey that wanders too close. Some individuals can be approached quite easily, but most are skittish.

GARDEN EELS (*Gorgasia sillneri*) belong to the conger eel family. Colonies of 100 to 1,000 or more individuals are found in sandy bottoms, at depths ranging from 10 to 80 feet. You will find them rising vertically out of their holes, looking like plants growing out of the sand, except that they move rhythmically, catching plankton brought their way by the currents. As you approach, they slowly retract into their lairs. Most published photographs of these shy creatures were taken from a blind; garden eels seem to value their personal space and generally will not allow an observer within 15 feet.

CORNETFISH (*Fistularia commersonii*) are usually found in shallow water, at depths of 30 feet and less. The slow-moving silvery fish have an elongated snout which is used to suck in prey. They can be approached for closeups if divers swim slowly and avoid threatening movements. Adult cornetfish are about two feet long, with a diameter of less than three inches.

Tiny PIPEFISH (Syngnathidae) look like miniature cornetfish, but are more closely related to seahorses. The male carries fertilized eggs in a brood pouch, where the young hatch. Look for them on reefs or sand in shallow water.

FLASHLIGHT FISH (*Photoblepharon palpebratus*) are among the most fascinating fishes in the Red Sea (see Chapter VII, Night Diving). They live in deep water or in caves by day but come near the surface at night, especially when there is no moon. Look for bright blue-green lights swimming about the reef like giant fireflies. Sometimes the lights go out momentarily, as the fish blinks its "eyelid" to hide the pouch under its eye that contains luminescent bacteria. It is best to follow them with your light out, then corner the fish and suddenly switch it on to get a good look. These shy fish usually swim in pairs. The Red Sea is one of the few places in the world where flashlight fish are found in water shallow enough to be seen by divers.

Sweetlips, Plectorhynchus gaterinus, *are common at the Pinnacles and at Ota Abu Rimata.*

Large jacks (Carangidae) often cruise the blue water near walls and reefs.

SQUIRRELFISHES (Holocentridae) are red-orange fish, about a foot long, with large eyes adapted for seeing at night. During the day they are found in caves or crevices; after dark they roam the reef looking for prey.

GROUPERS (Serrenidae) form one of the largest families of fishes, ranging in size from the giant *Promicrops lanceolatus,* which can grow in excess of 200 pounds, to the tiny *Anthias,* the ubiquitous goldfish about four inches in length. Most groupers have a protruding lower jaw with several rows of small, sharp teeth. The larger ones can suck in prey by suddenly opening their jaws, causing a partial vacuum and a sudden inrush of water. Larger groupers must be baited in for a close look. Medium sized ones, such as the 15 inch CORAL GROUPER, *Cephalopholis miniata,* are reef dwellers, generally hanging out in holes to ambush prey. A beautiful red fish with small blue spots, the Coral Grouper is a main course in many delicious meals on fishing boats. Other common intermediate size groupers are the Peacock Grouper, *Cephalopholis argus,* and the Smalltooth Grouper, *Epinephelus microdon.*

GOLDFISH (*Anthias sp.*) are often the most obvious fish on a

94

When a male Anthias *is removed, a dominant female will change sex and take his place.*

wall or reef; vast clouds of them flit about the scenery like so many butterflies. Feeding on tiny plankton, they begin adult life as females. When a dominant male is lost from the group, one of the larger females changes sex to take his place. Males, who may service a harem of up to 40 females, have purple markings, while the females remain orange. Goldfish can add life and interest to your wide-angle reef shots, or provide excellent closeups.

HAWKFISHES (Cirrhitidae) usually sit on top of small coral heads to ambush unwary prey. The Blackside Hawkfish, *Paracirrhites forsteri*, sits motionless on coral clumps and is one of the easiest of small reef denizens to approach closely and photograph.

One of the most beautifully colored fish in the Red Sea is the brilliant violet FRIDMAN FISH, *Pseudochromis fridmani*. This tiny two-inch fish belongs to the Dottyback family and is also known as the Orchid Dottyback. A 100 mm macro lens is needed to photograph it properly.

JACKS (Carangidae) in search of prey sometimes swarm in vast schools near walls or reefs adjacent to deep water. At Shark Reef near Ras Muhammed, the schools can be so dense that, from a

The masked butterflyfish, Chaetodon semilarvatus *, is unique to the Red Sea.*

distance, they look like another reef. While they hunt small fish, sharks often hunt the jacks. The large, silvery fish, called "bayad" in Arabic, are strong swimmers and are prized by fishermen for their fighting qualities as well as their good taste. Larger jacks can exceed two feet in length, and are approachable when hunting in small groups. The best way to get close is just to wait and let them come to you.

The smaller SNAPPERS, up to a foot in length, are also schooling fish. Swarms of Blueline Snapper, *Lutjanus coeruleolineatus*, are found at Ota Abu Rimata in the summer; large schools of Dory Snappers, *Lutjanus fulviflamma*, are common at Marsa Alam.

GRUNTS (Haemulidae) get their name from the noise they make by grinding the teeth in their pharynx. SWEETLIPS, *Plectorhynchus gaterinus*, are shallow- water grunts with black leopard spots on a silvery body, trimmed in yellow. They often occur in pairs or small schools of about a dozen, in and around reefs.

The BIGEYE EMPEROR, *Monotaxis grandoculis*, is a silvery fish with canine teeth, usually shy. At Ota Abu Rimata, however, they congregate in cleaning stations and can be approached quite

The emperor angelfish, Pomacanthus imperator, *is found throughout the Indo-Pacific.*

closely.

BATFISH, *Platax oricularis,* are about the size and shape of a large dinner plate. They hover in vast schools near Shark Reef. These inquisitive fish sometimes approach divers closely.

SILVER SWEEPERS, *Parapriacanthus guentheri,* tiny, almost transparent silvery fish, are found in vast schools, generally inside caves and around shipwrecks. They make photographers' eyes light up like strobes, because they make such beautiful frames for diver and scenic shots, as well as being fine subjects themselves. Try back-lighting the sweeper school with a second strobe, or just shoot the almost solid mass of fish with a single one to get the silvery effect. Be careful not to overexpose when using fill flash, because they reflect a lot of light. Another commonly used name for them is glassfish, because of the transparency of their bodies.

BARRACUDA (Sphyraenidae) are not included in the section on potentially dangerous creatures because the Red Sea varieties are not known to attack man. Even in other parts of the world, their fierce reputation is exaggerated unless you are a fish which forms part of their diet. The sleek, silvery fish often cruise slowly in schools

The orangestriped triggerfish, Balistapus undulatus, *is an aggressive creature, eating everything from live coral to sea urchins.*

near the surface around the reefs. To find them, look up occasionally when swimming over shallow reefs.

DAMSELFISHES (Pomacentridae) are among the most conspicuous fishes on a coral reef. Extremely territorial and usually colorful, they are favorites of underwater photographers and sightseers.

The TWOBAR ANEMONEFISH, *Amphiprion bicinctus*, the only clownfish in the Red Sea, is bright yellow orange with two white stripes that sometimes appear pale blue. A mucus secreted by the fish prevents the host anemone's nematocysts from discharging, allowing *Amphiprion* to find refuge from predators by retreating within its tentacles. The fish gains more from the symbiotic relationship than its host. The only benefits to the anemone are tactile stimulation, removal of some parasites, and perhaps some protection from coelenterate-eating fishes. All young anemonefish are males; one of them changes its sex when the largest female is removed.

Another damselfish, the DOMINO, *Dascyllus trimaculatus*, often shares an anemone with clownfish when it is young. Sometimes the tiny black fish, with a conspicuous white spot on its upper

The Rockskipper, Istiblennius edentulus, *can remain out of the water for hours, as long as its gills remain moist.*

back, is mistaken for a juvenile anemonefish.

The SERGEANT MAJOR, *Abudefduf saxitalis,* is found in shallow tropical waters all around the world. Although not as common in the Red Sea as in the Caribbean, large swarms often show up on Sinai beach dives when divers appear, especially if they bring food.

WRASSES (Labridae) are a diverse family, ranging in size from tiny cleaner fish two inches long to the giant NAPOLEON WRASSE, *Cheilinus undulatus.* Also called the Humphead Wrasse, this grotesque creature is the largest member of its family in the world, ranging up to 400 pounds. Its thick, fleshy lips, the bump on its head, the tiny eye, and the blue and green pattern on its face make this slow moving fish seem almost comical. Most prefer to keep their distance from divers, but others have been trained over a period of time to take food from the hand. Despite their size, the fish can be quite gentle and some individuals even allow themselves to be stroked and petted. For three years, a trained Napoleon, George, inhabited the Jolanda wreck and was fed regularly by dive guides. He would ingest hardboiled eggs and spit out pieces of the shell through his gills; parrotfish then zoomed in to eat the fragments. George disappeared not too long ago, but smaller Napoleons have been observed performing the same egg trick.

Many smaller wrasses are brilliantly colored, especially the juveniles. The CLEANER WRASSE, *Labroides dimidiatus*, eats parasites and dead tissue from the skin of other fish. Many predators, including moray eels, even allow the tiny fish to swim inside their mouth unharmed. An occasional imposter takes advantage of this trust. Colored like the cleaner wrasse, the MIMIC BLENNY, *Aspidontus taeniatus,* nips living bits of flesh from the fins of fish expecting to be cleaned. Most wrasses begin life as females; some undergo a sex change to become males when they reach adulthood.

PARROTFISHES (Scaridae) have large fused front teeth which are used to scrape corals and rock surfaces so they can eat the algae growing there. They are usually seen in shallow water, chewing coral rock and defecating coral sand. Parrotfish are among the major sand producers on a reef. At night they find refuge in small crevices within the reef to sleep. Many of them secrete a mucous cocoon that offers protection from parasites and predators. During the day, parrotfish generally prefer a personal space of three to four feet from a diver, just out of range of good photographs. But at night the camera can be placed almost on the sleeper's nose.

Another common and brightly decorated family of reef fishes is the BUTTERFLYFISH (Chaedontidae). Some of them are night feeders, only semi active during daylight hours and easily approachable. Most of the time they swim in pairs, but at Ota Abu Rimata they form large aggregations. Among the most colorful are the MASKED BUTTERFLYFISH, *Chaetodon semilarvatus*, the CROWN BUTTERFLYFISH, *Chaetodon paucifasciatus*, and the STRIPED BUTTERFLYFISH, *Chaetodon fasciatus*. The RED SEA BANNERFISH, *Heniochus intermedius*, resembles a moorish idol because of its dorsal crest, but is actually a butterflyfish.

All around the world, ANGELFISHES (Pomacathidae) are perhaps the most admired and beautiful denizens of coral reefs. The Red Sea is no exception, with three dazzling species heading the list. The YELLOWBAR ANGELFISH, *Pomacanthus maculosis* has a royal blue body with a large yellow mark on its side which resembles

Crocodile fish, Cociella crocodila, *are ambush predators, usually found in sandy areas.*

a map of Africa. Local divers refer to it as the Mapfish. The EMPEROR ANGELFISH, *Pomacanthus imperator* has alternating blue and yellow horizontal bands on its body with a black mask, outlined in electric blue. It is a difficult fish to photograph well, because correct exposure on the bright body means loss of detail on the dark mask and eye. The ROYAL ANGELFISH, *Pygoplites diacanthus*, has a vertical pattern of blue and white bars on a yellow body. As beautiful as the adults are, juveniles have even brighter patterns and colors.

SURGEONFISHES (Acanthuridae) often swim in vast schools in the open water around a reef, in the upper 40 feet of the water column. One or more sharp barbs at the base of the tail are used to slash predators, including careless divers. The BLACK SURGEON-FISH, *Acanthuris nigricans*, occasionally displays vertical white bands across its face, perhaps connected with a courting ritual. The BLUESPINE UNICORNFISH, *Naso unicornis*, gets its name from a single horn which projects horizontally from its forehead. Its cousin, *Naso brevirostris*, has an even more elongated schnozz which lends a comical look.

BLENNIES (Bleniidae) are tiny fish which generally hide in holes. But the ROCKSKIPPER, *Istiblennius edentulus*, spends a lot of time on land. In tidepools or on sandy shores, this little fish out of water hops on top of rocks to eat algae and perhaps to escape predators. Studies have shown they can spend up to five hours out of the water.

TRIGGERFISHES (Balistidae) are oddly shaped creatures with compressed bodies, long snouts, and often striking coloration. During the summer, males are often seen hovering vertically over the sand, guarding their mate's eggs. They also feed by blowing sand away to uncover buried creatures. When a diver approaches they become quite aggressive, charging with teeth bared and occasionally even biting a fin. The TITAN TRIGGERFISH, *Balistoides viridescens*, and the BLUE TRIGGERFISH, *Pseudobalistes fuscus*, are likely to display this sort of behavior, and at two feet in length, they can be intimidating. Among the smaller ones, the shy PICASSO TRIGGERFISH, *Rhinecanthus assasi*, has exceptionally beautiful markings, as does the more aggressive ORANGESTRIPED TRIGGERFISH, *Balistapus undulatus*.

The silvertip shark, Carcharhinus albimarginatus, *usually keeps its distance from divers.*

PUFFERS (Tetraodontidae) can swell their bodies by drawing in water, thus making them too large a mouthful for many predators. In addition, some of their internal organs are extremely toxic, so eating one can be hazardous to the predator's health. The MASKED PUFFER, *Arothron diadematus*, and the BRISTLY PUFFER, *Arothron hispidus*, are two of the most common species. Both are slow-moving fish, easily photographed. PORCUPINE FISHES (Diodontidae) are similar,except they add sharp spines all around their body to their arsenal of defensive weapons.

Among the SOLES (Soleidae), the tiny MOSES SOLE (*Pardachirus marmoratus*) has received the most attention for the mucus it secretes, which has been found to repel sharks. Usually buried in the sand, this flatfish swims about a foot when disturbed, then buries itself again by vibrating its body to agitate the sand. It remains there while a diver fans the sand away, perhaps thinking its camouflage or poison will discourage the persistent nuisance. If touched, the sole repeats the short swim and burial procedure.

Another interesting sand dweller is the CROCODILE FISH, *Cociella crocodila*, belonging to the family Platycephalidae. A master of camouflage, this flat-bodied fish waits in ambush for unwary prey. When moving to rocks or coral, it rapidly changes color pattern to match the new surroundings. Although some individuals are shy, crocodile fish often pose passively for closeup pictures. Be careful not to overexpose the sand bottom.

POTENTIALLY DANGEROUS CREATURES

In the Red Sea, as in most oceans of the world, the dangerous creatures are generally unagressive toward man. Only when placed in a fight or flight situation do they pose a problem. The dangers of the underwater world are largely in peoples' minds, nurtured by the sensationalism of the media. After all, shy sharks don't sell deodorant on television. It would be a shame to miss some of the sights and sensations of the underwater world because of ambiguous fears.

Still, a prudent diver needs knowledge of creatures to avoid potentially dangerous situations. Some pose more risk than others. An inadvertent brush against fire coral can result in itching and

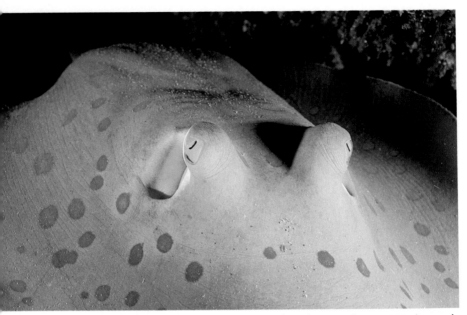

The beautiful blue-spotted stingray, Taeniura lymma, *is common in sandy areas, or under small coral heads.*

burning skin for several days. An inadvertent brush with a stonefish can result in death. The purpose of this section is to inform the reader of possible dangers so he or she will know when to be cautious.

After nearly 300 dives in the Red Sea, I have no real SHARK stories to tell. Sharks were observed on less than 10 percent of the dives, but in nearly every case they maintained a respectful distance of 30 feet or more and promptly disappeared into the blue. Often only the first diver in the water saw the animals. To sharks, divers probably look like big, ugly, dangerous beasts.

Dive guide Rolf Schmidt observed that the shark population in Sinai seems to have diminished since 1980. This is a bit strange because the years from 1978 to 1982 were the period of heaviest diver pressure. Also, there is very little fishing for sharks. He feels this is part of a natural cycle, and expects the numbers to eventually return to the level of earlier days.

It is common to see nurse sharks resting in the sand. At some locations white tips, gray reef sharks, and hammerheads can be seen cruising in open water. Six families of sharks are normally found in the Red Sea: nurse sharks (Orectoblidae), the whale shark (Rhinocondontidae), thresher sharks (Alopiidae), mackerel sharks (Isuri-

Covered with marine growth, the stonefish resembles a rock with a frown.

dae), requiem sharks (Charcharhinidae), and hammerheads (Sphyrnidae). The Great White Shark has not been reported here.

Unless a shark displays aggressive behavior, no particular caution is called for. If it circles, arches its back with pectoral fins lowered, or makes sudden spasmodic movements, the best strategy is to beat a hasty but dignified retreat without turning your back. Avoid any quick movements which could be construed as aggressive or panicky.

Several species of rays are common in the Red Sea. There is a small ELECTRIC RAY, *Torpedo marmorata*, usually no more than a foot in diameter. It is often buried in the sand and can deliver a fairly strong shock if touched. Colored a mottled brown, this little creature is well camouflaged.

STINGRAYS range in size from those having a wingspan of about a foot, such as the reef, or blue spotted stingray (*Taeniura lymma*) to the eagle ray (*Myliobatis aquila*), which grows to four feet or more. All have one or more venomous spines near the base of their tail which are used for defense when they are cornered or frightened. The sting is extremely painful and temporarily debilitating. One Hurghada dive guide suffered a serious injury when he was

105

A well-camouflaged, venomous scorpionfish, Scorpaenopsis oxycephalus, *lies in ambush, waiting for a meal. Scorpionfishes are often mistaken for stonefish.*

stung on the neck attempting to feed a stingray. However, these docile creatures never attack; they usually swim away when disturbed.

The BLUE SPOTTED RAY is usually found in sandy areas or hiding beneath small table corals. An excellent photographic subject, this beautiful animal can sometimes be approached very closely for dramatic pictures. Just move slowly and try not to disturb it. If the ray is skittish it will swim rapidly to another shelter, but sometimes it just lies there and submits to half a dozen flash pictures before moving.

STONEFISH (*Synancia verrucosa*) are not very common in the Red Sea, and their nearly perfect camouflage renders them virtually invisible. Most people who claim to have seen one were probably looking at a scorpionfish. The actual stonefish lives in coral crevices in shallow sandy areas, and looks like a rock with a frown. It is the downturned mouth that's the tipoff. Probably the most venomous fish in the world, wounds from its spines are extremely painful and have been known to result in death. Be careful when walking over reefs, shuffle your feet, and wear boots with substantial soles. They

106

For the small fish and invertebrates that are its prey, this view of Pterois volitans *could be the last thing they ever see.*

are not aggressive toward people, and will usually remain motionless while being poked or prodded. Use a snorkel or a piece of coral for this maneuver. If you aren't sure about a fish, don't touch it.

SCORPIONFISH (Scorpaenopsis) are also camouflage experts, preferring to hide motionless in holes or under corals to ambush prey. At night they sometimes lie in the open on the reef. The spines on the dorsal and pectoral fins are venomous, causing swelling and severe pain. A diver would almost have to lean on one to get stung, because they just don't move. A camera may be placed practically on its nose, and even an electronic flash doesn't upset it. If you do get stung, immerse the injury in water as hot as you can stand. Heat denatures the protein material of the venom.

An old saying among divers is, "If it's ugly, don't touch it". The LIONFISH is an exception to the rule, because it is one of the most beautiful fish in the sea. It is also one of the most venomous, the sting causing excruciating pain and even some fatalities. Two species are common in the Red Sea. *Pterois volitans* is sometimes called the zebrafish, turkeyfish or firefish. The enlarged pectoral fins look like wings. These fish often swim slowly just off the bottom and, when

107

Pterois radiata *usually hides in crevices, and is not as active as its cousin,* Pterois volitans.

threatened, usually turn their back, pointing their venomous fins at the enemy. However, some of them seem to become used to humans and just continue to swim slowly and calmly. In those cases, they make great photographic subjects. Sometimes a resting lionfish doesn't move at all, allowing outstanding closeup shots. Just be careful of others hovering around you.

Pterois radiata has long, graceful spines, without a membrane between them, that look like rays. This lionfish is more skittish than *volitans*, and is usually found in holes. It turns its back toward divers on nearly every encounter, and is usually photographed from behind. In order to tease it out use a knife or a snorkel, because there is no safe way to manipulate this creature by hand.

MORAY EELS are common throughout the Red Sea, but are dangerous only when mishandled. The largest is the giant moray (*Gymnothorax javanicus*) which can attain a length of over six feet. Although they can be trained to accept food by hand and even be embraced and petted, such activities are best left to the dive guides who can recognize individuals.

FIRE CORAL (Millepora) is found in most of the world's tropical seas. Not a true coral, Millepora is a hydroid that grows in a

Gymnothorax javanicus is the largest moray in the Indo-pacific region.

yellowish mass over true corals, assuming a similar shape. Close inspection will reveal tiny hairlike projections. These contain nematocysts, or stinging cells which do the damage. When brushing against fire coral an immediate stinging, burning sensation is felt. The severity of symptoms depends upon the victim's sensitivity to the toxin. Sometimes a rash will develop that can itch periodically for several weeks after initial exposure. Wearing a wetsuit and gloves will prevent contact with the nematocysts when kneeling or leaning on fire coral. If you do get stung, immediate application of meat tenderizer will often relieve all symptoms. Mix the powder with water to make a paste, and put it directly on the sting. Enzymes in the meat tenderizer break down the proteins in the venom to neutralize its effect.

SEA URCHINS are rarely seen during the day; most of the Red Sea's species are nocturnal. Be careful where you kneel or place your hand on night dives, because an encounter with these seagoing pincushions can be painful. *Diadema* has long, sharp, brittle spines that can penetrate a wetsuit and break off in the skin. Treat sea urchin wounds as you would a splinter and attempt to remove the spine with a sterilized needle and tweezers. Try to pull it straight out to avoid breaking it. If that happens, it sometimes helps to soak the injury in vinegar. The acetic acid can dissolve the calcium carbonate spine.

A short spined sea-urchin, *Asthenosoma varium*, colored bright red with spherical sacs longer than its spines, is a common sight on the reefs at night. These sacs contain a strong poison that can cause severe pain.

Several varieties of CONE SHELLS are found in the Red Sea. The small mollusc living inside has a barbed radula which can inject a powerful poison. It is illegal to collect living specimens, so if you follow the law you are unlikely to experience difficulty. When handling it for other reasons, hold it by the sides and keep your fingers away from the shell opening.

The Red Sea is a relatively benign place and its few hazards connected with marine life are easily avoided. Exercise prudent respect, but there is no reason to fear looking and touching. After all, that's an important part of the fun of diving.

Index to Marine Life Photographs

The reader may wish to use the marine life photographs in this book to identify creatures observed underwater. Because the pictures are placed to match the text, without regard to scientific classifications, an index is helpful to find a specific photograph. Two indexes are presented here. One is based on popular names, the other on scientific names. Both are divided into vertebrate and invertebrate sections. Only those photographs whose captions identify an animal are listed.

Scientific Names
Invertebrates

Vertebrates

Adioryx spinifer	122	*Istiblennius edentulus*	99
Amphiprion bicinctus	69	*Oxycirrhites typus*	183
Anthias sp.	79, 95	*Parapriacanthus guentheri*	82, 159, 161
Arothron diadematus	187	*Photoblepheron palpebratus*	198
Balistapus undulatus	98	*Plectorhynchus gaterinus*	93
Balistoides viridescens	52	*Pomacanthus imperator*	97
Carangidae	94	*Pomacanthus maculosis*	81
Carcharhinus albimarginatus	102	*Pterois radiata*	108
Cephalopholis miniata	166	*Pterois volitans*	107, 150
Chaetodon semilarvatus	52, 96	*Scorpaenopsis oxycephalus*	106
Cheilinus undulatus	72, 162	*Synanceia verrucosa*	84, 105, 141
Cociella crocodila	101	*Taeniura lymma*	104
Gymnothorax javanicus	109		

Popular Names

Invertebrates

Basket star	196	Hermit crab	164
Cassiopeia jellyfish	167	Plate coral	78
Crinoids	185	Red Coral crab	192
Crown of Thorns	89	Sea urchin	196
Cup coral	77	Soft coral	87, 138, 163
Cuttlefish	194	Spanish Dancer	199, 201
Decorator crab	91	Spider crab	192
Giant clam	90	Starfish	68, 88

Vertebrates

Blue-spotted stingray	104	Masked puffer	187
Clownfish	69	Moray eel	109
Coral grouper	166	Napoleon wrasse	72, 162
Crocodile fish	101	Orangestriped triggerfish	98
Emperor Angelfish	97	Rockskipper	99
Flashlight fish	198	Scorpionfish	106
Goldfish	79, 95	Sea turtle	120, 178
Grouper	155	Silver sweepers	82, 159, 161
Jacks	94	Silvertip shark	102
Lionfish (*P. radiata*)	108	Squirrelfish	122
Lionfish (*P.volitans*)	107, 150	Stonefish	84, 105, 141
Longnose hawkfish	183	Sweetlips	93
Mapfish	81	Titan triggerfish	52
Masked butterflyfish	59, 96	Tuna	156

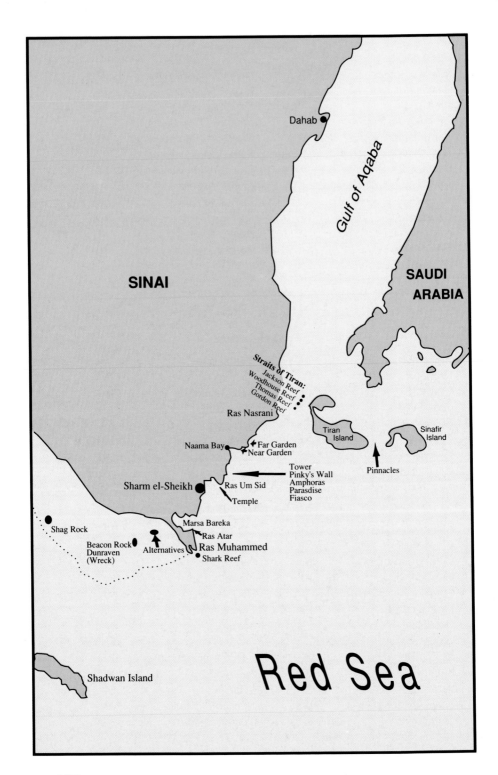

Dahab

Gulf of Aqaba

SINAI

SAUDI ARABIA

Straits of Tiran:
Jackson Reef
Woodhouse Reef
Thomas Reef
Gordon Reef

Ras Nasrani

Tiran Island

Sinafir Island

Naama Bay
Far Garden
Near Garden

Tower
Pinky's Wall
Amphoras
Parasdise
Fiasco

Pinnacles

Sharm el-Sheikh
Ras Um Sid

Temple

Marsa Bareka

Shag Rock

Ras Atar

Beacon Rock
Dunraven
(Wreck)

Alternatives

Ras Muhammed
Shark Reef

Shadwan Island

Red Sea

112

Chapter 5

Sinai

Sinai. The name alone speaks volumes of history. In ancient Egyptian mythology, the goddess Isis crossed Sinai in her search for the body of her murdered husband, Osiris. The Israelites crossed the Red Sea here, fleeing the Pharaoh's troops. Moses received the Ten Commandments on Mount Sinai. Saladin fought the Crusaders here in the Middle Ages. The Turks swept across the peninsula in the sixteenth century to conquer Egypt. The wars of 1967 and 1973 between Egypt and Israel were fought on its sands.

When seeing the Sinai today you realize how a modern army could conquer the peninsula just as quickly as a half track can move across its desert sands. But besides the desert, there are also high mountains, oases and orchards, historic monasteries, and lovely beaches. In Pharaonic times, gold, copper and turquoise were mined there. Today it is a rich source of oil.

Sinai has always been a vital link connecting the continents of Europe, Africa and Asia. It has also provided a buffer zone between Egypt and its potential enemies. When the 1979 peace treaty with Israel returned the Sinai to Egyptian control, the Multinational Force and Observers (MFO) was created. An international military force consisting mostly of American troops, it is stationed there indefinitely to keep the peace.

Sinai is still a frontier in a harsh desert environment. Transportation and communication can be difficult. Water is scarce. But after a period of dormancy, a construction boom in the late 80s is bringing exciting new facilities for tourists and divers. In terms of efficiency, convenience, and comfort, the new hotels, dive centers, and boats are 20 years ahead of what was there before. And above all, the reefs are healthy — perhaps healthier than they have been in several years — because there was less diver pressure during the first five years of Egyptian rule.

Most diving in the region is land-based from Naama Bay, just north of the town of Sharm El Sheikh. There is also a dive center at Dahab and one at Nuweiba, although the latter was closed when this book was written. The dive sites here are divided into four sectors: Northern Sinai, Naama Bay, Ras Muhammed and the Straits of Tiran.

NORTHERN SINAI

Diving access to the northern Gulf of Aqaba is through the diving centers at Nuweiba and Dahab. Both had been extremely dependent upon tourists from Israel for the bulk of their business, as most international visitors concentrate on Naama Bay. At the time of our last visit, the NUWEIBA operation was closed so we couldn't dive this area. Those sites are covered in detail in Shlomo Cohen's *Red Sea Diver's Guide*. Anyone interested in diving there should look up that publication.

DAHAB has two small Bedouin villages and some of the most beautiful white sand beaches in Sinai. It has become a haven for backpackers and young travelers on low budgets, who live in thatched huts by the seashore for very low rent. The Bedouins, a proud nomadic people who claim allegiance to no country, eke out an existence as herdsmen and traders while they move about the area. Although their homes are little more than plywood shacks with goats and camels roaming through the front yards, the villagers possess an inordinate number of Mercedes and Jeeps.

One dive center is located in Dahab, but it doesn't offer all the services and facilities of the Naama Bay centers. Most persons who dive there are locals, Israelis, or expatriates living in Egypt. It

8,000 feet above the desert floor, hikers watch the sunrise from the top of Mount Sinai. Egyptians call it Moses Mountain.

ST. CATHERINE'S MONASTERY AND MOSES MOUNTAIN

When the Sinai was returned to Egypt, President Anwar Sadat had a retreat built for himself at the foot of Mount Sinai. It was meant to serve as Egypt's Camp David, a place for the chief executive to get away from the hectic pace of the capitol and entertain guests of state. Unfortunately, he was able to enjoy it for only one visit before his assassination by extremists in 1981.

Located on a plateau 5,100 feet above sea level, it is one of the most spectacular places in Egypt. In the crisp air, the surrounding mountains look close enough to touch. Their stark peaks are shrouded with snow in winter.

Natural springs make it possible for fruit orchards to grow, and temperatures are cool when contrasted with the heat of the desert. A modern resort, with room for 200 guests, is located there, constructed from granite rocks to retain the environmental atmosphere of the area.

ST. CATHERINE'S MONASTERY
AND MOSES MOUNTAIN (con't)

St. Catherine's Monastery dates back to the 6th century, during the reign of the Emperor Justinian. It honors the daughter of one of Alexandria's rulers, who was tortured to death for her conversion to Christianity. Like a medieval fortress, the old churches and living quarters for the Greek Orthodox monks are surrounded by a 35-foot wall. Justinian began construction of The Basilica in 527, making it one of the oldest Christian churches still standing. It encompasses the site of the Chapel of the Burning Bush, built 100 years earlier by Emperor Constantine, on the spot where God spoke to Moses. Visitors are allowed into the monastery only during specified hours which won't interfere with the activities of the monks. Schedules are posted at the gate.

From the monastery you can begin the three-hour climb of Mount Sinai, or Moses Mountain as it is known by the Egyptians. It was here that the prophet — who is revered by Muslims as well as Christians and Jews — received the Ten Commandments. The climb is usually begun around 2 AM so that you can watch the sun rise from the mountaintop. Your Bedouin guide will lead you up a gradual incline, with many switchbacks intended to ease the climb. We did it by the light of a full moon, but flashlights will be necessary on a dark night. Wear comfortable shoes and bring a jacket, because it's cold and windy on the top at 7,500 feet. Watching the sun rise over layers of mountains from one of the highest peaks in Egypt is well worth the trip. You may descend by a more direct route over some 2,000 stone steps hewn into the mountain. It would be extremely difficult going up this way, and even coming down, the stress is felt in your legs. The stairway ends in back of the monastery.

No matter how tired you are from the climb, reach back for that last bit of energy and climb a couple of hundred yards up the cliff opposite the front of the monastery. It affords a beautiful view of the buildings inside the wall, and of the mountain you just climbed. Don't forget your camera.

St. Catherine's Monastery dates back to the sixth century. Originally a Coptic church, it is operated today by Greek Orthodox monks.

is possible to rent a Bedouin taxi for the day to make the 130-mile round trip from Sharm El Sheikh. Prices are negotiable, and the driver will take you directly to the dive site and wait for you while you dive.

Diving is done from the beaches, with short walks over coral reefs to reach the dropoffs. The narrow Gulf of Aqaba funnels the prevailing north winds, so entries at Dahab are almost always made through wind chop. With the exception of a few Napoleons and groupers, big fish here are rare, the legacy of unregulated spearfishing in years past. Reef fish, however, remain abundant.

The most popular dive site in the region is THE CANYON, a coral passage leading from shallow water to an exit at 160 feet. Only advanced divers should attempt this dive. From the entry point, follow the sand channel straight out, then over the reeftop to the right. Turn left and follow the reef, looking south (right) at the sand below for a beehive-shaped coral head at 45 feet. This is the upper entrance to the open coral tunnel that forms the canyon. Entry is through the "beehive", or directly through the tunnel some 15 feet below, into the main chamber of the canyon itself. The contrast between the confines of the tunnel and the vast chamber with its "skylight" create feelings on which to build a dive. The canyon is actually an incomplete coral cave with a slot in the roof that admits some light. Extending up to 30 feet above the ceiling in most places, the slot is too narrow for a diver to fit through. The canyon winds and twists through the reef to its exit point at a depth of 160 feet. Be sure to check your bottom time and air supply if you plan to follow it all the way, a swim of some 200 feet down the sloping tunnel. The slope becomes steeper the further you penetrate, and safety decompression will be necessary when you ascend the outside wall. Some divers may prefer to swim the cave a short distance, then return and exit from the starting point. Sinai veterans say this was a more beautiful dive years ago, when the entrance was filled with lush invertebrate growth. Today all you will see are glassy sweepers near the entrance, and a few plate corals and sponges inside. Besides the sweepers there are few photo opportunities; this is primarily an experience dive.

Dahab's other renowned dive site is the BLUE HOLE. Like the Canyon, this is for advanced divers only. About 1.4 miles north

Beach diving in Sinai entails short walks over shallow fringing reefs, then a step off into the clear blue water.

118

A CAMEL DIVE

If you are looking for a different experience, how about riding a camel to the dive site? That's the way people dive RAS ABU GALUM, about nine miles north of Dahab. Make arrangements for the trip through the local dive center. Although the first three miles are covered by car, the rest of the dirt road is too narrow, so the site can be reached only on the back of a camel. The beasts are rented from the local Bedouins, who serve as animal handlers and guides. Camels are called Ships of the Desert for good reason. When riding one, you sway with its rhythm to avoid discomfort.

The dive itself features a sandy entry, with beautiful corals and invertebrates, but little fish activity. However, the trip is a mini adventure which will put you one up on your friends when it's story-telling time.

of The Canyon on a dirt road, it is a large hole in the reef that drops vertically to a sand bottom at a reported depth of over 300 feet. Across the top, the hole measures about 50 meters, then narrows as you go deeper. Inside, it is relatively barren, with few fish and considerable sediment, however the large plate corals along the walls are exceptional. A high, arching passage leads through the reef to open water, beginning at a depth of 165 feet. Around 36 feet in length, the passage lies almost due north of the entry point. It looks like the door of a blue mosque, especially under the influence of nitrogen. To make this dive safely, a diver should have at least two thirds of his air supply remaining when entering the passage. There isn't time to search. If you don't find the passage immediately, the recommended procedure is to ascend inside the hole, then swim over the 25-foot seaward sill to the wall, and finish the dive there in shallow water for safety decompression. Or else you can make a deep dive on the wall east of the blue hole, then swim over the reef at twenty feet and decompress within the hole. The outer wall is the best in the Dahab area, with lush, yellow soft corals and lots of reef fish activity.

Sea turtles often swim in blue water along walls and dropoffs. Divers can sometimes approach very closely.

The EEL GARDEN is a sandy slope dropping gently from 20 feet to over 100 feet. Full of garden eels, it is one of the best places in the Red Sea to observe these shy creatures. Late in the afternoon, if the sun is in the right place, a diver can approach closely before they retract into their holes. The area is interspersed with small coral heads which harbor Spanish Dancers. Often these nocturnal nudibranchs can even be seen by day, if you look carefully into small holes and crevices.

The LIGHTHOUSE is another once popular area which has succumbed to too much diver pressure. Entry is south of the lighthouse. Heading north along the reef, the diver will reach a wall that drops off to 130 feet. However, many of the corals have been broken; this is one of the most worn-out reefs on the Sinai coast.

The ISLAND lies some 50 yards offshore, a submerged reef with a maximum depth of 35 feet. Located in an area of strong water movement, it has excellent hard corals and lots of reef fish. Schools of barracuda are often seen hovering overhead.

STRAITS OF TIRAN

Accessible only by boat, the Straits of Tiran and Tiran Islands guard the entrance to the Gulf of Aqaba. They consist of three islands and a series of coral reefs, all interesting areas to dive. The reefs can be reached by day boat from Naama Bay, while the islands generally require an overnight trip. However, because of political tensions between Egypt and Saudi Arabia, the islands are sometimes declared off limits to divers. Check at the dive center for the current status.

Tiran, the largest of the three islands, is the only one belonging to Egypt. A military outpost is located there, but the troops generally don't interfere with diving activities. KUSH KASH-KAR, located on the southwest corner, is a convenient anchorage and a good place for a first night dive in the Red Sea. A short wall drops to a sand shelf at 25 feet, then slopes to a sand plateau at 100 feet. It continues deeper in a series of steps, surrounded by the rock walls of a gradually narrowing canyon. In shallow water, coral outcrops house reef fish by day, with an occasional crocodile fish in the sand. At night, the typical mixture of nocturnal creatures is present.

CORAL GARDENS drops to a 40 foot sand bottom with large coral clumps, one of which reaches the surface. The remains of an ancient fishing boat, about 500 years old, are embedded in the sand. Small bits of pottery and a wooden keel, heavily overgrown, can still be seen. Crocodile fish, blue spotted stingrays and morays live among the outcrops, while eagle rays, turtles and Napoleons often swim by. This area is protected from currents, and is also a good site for night diving.

ROCK POINT, the southernmost tip of Tiran Island, offers no place for a vessel to secure, so this is a drift dive. The best area is shallow, above 50 feet. Below that point there is little of interest, except for the possibility of seeing some big fish. The wall slopes gradually, with big coral outcrops from 15 to 20 feet in depth. Small caves honeycomb the wall, many full of sweepers. Whitetip sharks and turtles sometimes frequent the area.

Between Tiran and Sinafir Islands lie THE PINNACLES, a reef system consisting of seven coral heads rising from a flat,

Squirrelfish, Adiorix Spinifer, *generally hide in dark crevices during the day.*

grassy sea bed in 35 feet of water. The four primary pinnacles form a circle about 50 meters across; a series of satellites head off toward Tiran Island. Often the site of strong currents, the rich soft coral growth is the result of abundant plankton in the water column. That reduces visibility somewhat in the summer months; the best time to dive this area is October through April. This is an outstanding area for photographing fish and observing their behavior. You will find large schools of one species that have staked out an area on a reef. So as you swim around a pinnacle you might first encounter a school of bannerfish, then emperorfish, then sweetlips, and perhaps finish in a small crevice filled with lionfish or silver sweepers. Most fish seem calm and unperturbed, probably because this area is seldom visited by divers.

The Pinnacles is one of the few places to catch a glimpse of the rare Red Sea dugong (a close relative of the manatee) swimming in the sea grass. Look there for sea horses as well. Don't forget to cruise the sand for crocodile fish, blue-spotted stingrays, and nurse sharks. Turtles and large moray eels are also seen regularly, as are eagle rays and large schools of barracuda. It's a good night diving spot for advanced divers, but difficult when strong winds blow from the north.

Sinafir Island, located in Saudi Arabian territory, was off limits to diving activity at the time this was written. Its outstanding site, THE MUSEUM, is located off the southeastern tip. Many ancient amphoras, estimated to be over a thousand years of age, lie embedded in the coral. Although located all around the reef, the nearly overgrown amphoras are hard to spot without a guide.

The main reef, which starts at 30 feet and drops down a gentle slope to 130 feet on the outside, is long and rectangular. Generally dead and colorless, it reminds one of a moonscape. The shoreward side is a different story, with superb soft corals and sea fans. Three canyons cut through the reef, their rich gorgonian growth providing great frames for diver pictures.

Starting in April and May, large schools of sweetlips hover around the reef, including the red sweetlips, rare in this area. Sleeping sharks, turtles, manta rays and schools of barracuda are also likely to be encountered here. As usual in areas with lush invertebrate growth, uncomfortably strong currents are sometimes present. Check at the dive center whether or not diving is allowed there at the time of your visit.

Four large coral reefs stand between the islands and the Sinai coast, lined up north to south. They comprise the STRAITS OF TIRAN, a navigable passage only about 800 meters wide yet 760 meters deep.

The northernmost site, JACKSON REEF, is marked by a large freighter which has run aground on its northern end. Dive guides rate the corals and reef fish at the southern end of Jackson second only to Ras Muhammed in the Sinai area. It is like a circus of fish, all competing for your attention; you hardly know where to turn next. Shallow water photographic opportunities are outstanding, especially over the vast field of fire coral trees on top of the reef. Dense schools of goldfish flit around the coral heads, while scorpionfish can be found in crevices. In the sandy patches look for small blacktip groupers, about a foot long. These docile, curious fish will swim right up to a reclining diver, staring into his mask. Sergeant majors, angels, butterflyfish, parrotfish, and triggerfish will vie for

The strong currents at Thomas Reef are responsible for the rich growth of sea fans and soft corals.

From 60 feet on Ras Muhammed Wall, you can see the surf breaking on the reef, while Anthias flit all around.

your attention as well, while schools of jacks darken the water overhead. The soft corals are outstanding, among the richest in Sinai.

The southern wall, which slopes to 200 feet, is the site of several large black coral trees. You don't have to go that deep to see sharks. The meeting of the currents between Jackson and Woodhouse reefs is called the SHARK LOOKOUT. There is a line attached to the reef at 80 feet, which you can hang onto in the current while observing the open water for sharks. White and blacktips, hammerheads and leopard sharks might be encountered. Strong currents often accompany tidal changes funneling through the straits. When they are present, this is an advanced dive. Jackson Reef is usually dived in the morning, when the north wind keeps the moored boat clear of the reef.

WOODHOUSE, a long, narrow reef, is seldom dived. When it is, it is done as a drift dive because there is no anchorage. The eastern side is a steep dropoff to about 130 feet, then sloping gradually into sand. Because this side is protected from currents, there are fewer soft corals. Large gray tube sponges project from the wall. Fish life consists mostly of reef fish, although eagle rays, sharks, and turtles sometimes cruise along the wall. At 120 feet is a small satellite reef, separated from the main one by a narrow canyon. Several holes continue downward through the canyon floor. At the ends of the reef strong currents can be encountered, bringing food to the large sea fans found there. Weather permitting, the outside is the better area, with a large overhang, large black coral trees, and several caves.

Like Woodhouse, THOMAS REEF is an advanced dive because there is no place to hide from the currents. It is also a drift dive, and can be done only when there are no strong winds. Starting at the southeastern end, swim counterclockwise to maximize favorable current exposure. As you circumnavigate this, the smallest of the Tiran reefs, there will be times the current is with you and times it goes against you. At the corners it is especially strong, giving the diver a feeling of flying along the wall. But check with your dive guide for conditions on any given day. There

The Lady Jenny V sets off into a Sinai sunset.

125

LIVE-ABOARD BOATS

Many veteran divers claim that a live-aboard boat is the best way to dive. In it, you can reach remote sites that are unattainable on day trips. It certainly frees you from all concerns except eating, sleeping, and diving. Most of the labor and hassle of frontier diving is absent as the crew drops you on the site, fills tanks, cooks, and cleans up while all you do is loaf, read, eat some more, and set up your diving and camera gear. Diving in the Red Sea is not unlimited, however. Owing to the depths, the routine usually consists of two to three dives during the day, and a final one at night. Long surface intervals are important for safety.

During the winter, over a dozen live-aboard dive boats ply the waters of Sinai. Fewer remain in summer, although more are planned for the near future. They range in length from 50 to over 100 feet, and feature air-conditioned state-rooms, large galleys, a shaded lower deck and a sundeck. A skiff or an inflatable boat usually takes divers to reefs away from the anchorage.

Food is good and plentiful. Although the fresh water supply is finite, there is plenty for washing bodies and equipment. There is electricity for charging strobes, and some even have a darkroom for processing E-6 film.

Most divemasters run a laissez-faire operation. If you need a guide, they provide the service. But if you have demonstrated competence and would rather go off with your buddy, they don't mind. There is usually no formal checkout, but on your first dive they will watch carefully to see how well you handle yourself.

Those boats departing from Eilat, Israel, sail overnight to Naama Bay and Ras Muhammed. The ones based in Sharm El Sheikh concentrate on southern Sinai and often venture into the Straits of Gubal, including Shadwan and Abu Nuhas.

All but the most diehard diving fanatics will realize that they are missing something by not seeing the country. However, a land tour can be arranged through the agency that booked the boat trip.

is no need to go deep; the best scenery is at about the 30 to 60 foot level. Because of the currents, soft corals and sea fans are outstanding. The wall is sheer, with many coral outcrops and overhangs. Be sure to look to outside water occasionally for cruising sharks, jacks, and tunas. This is one of the best places in the Red Sea to observe sharks, usually cruising about 30 feet below the diver. As you move around the reef out of the high current area, the scenery will change as the soft corals give way to a seascape dominated by fire corals on the south-facing side. A network of shallow caves, from 40 feet to the surface, house colorful fish and invertebrates. This is an exciting, high-energy dive; some guides rate it the best in the area.

GORDON REEF, a big flat formation, is usually done as an afternoon dive because of its shallow area. A freighter has run aground on the north end and looks as though it is parked there, just like the one on Jackson Reef. The reeftop is protected from currents, so topography is dominated by small outcrops and table corals. Look for small gray morays in crevices. Occasional sharks may swim through the area. Cargo from a 1950s shipwreck is scattered about the reef. On the east side, the maximum depth is 65 feet at the edge of the dropoff, while the southern end slopes gently to only 30 feet some 50 yards from the reef. The east side offers better scenery. This is a good night dive when there is no wind.

NAAMA BAY AND VICINITY

Naama Bay is a small tourist community just north of the town of Sharm El Sheikh. Formerly known only to diving enthusiasts, it has been discovered by Egyptians and Europeans seeking a beach resort and a base from which to explore Sinai. Three new hotels were built during 1987, featuring ameneties like swimming pools, restaurants and snack bars, even a disco and a pizzeria. Three new dive centers, as well as three dating back to the Israeli period, offer a wide scope of services ranging from beach dives and safari trips to day boats and live-aboards. These provide access to The Straits of Tiran and Ras Muhammed, as well as to the coastline. Winter is high season, when advance reservations are necessary. Summers used to be slow, but this is no longer the case. Although it may be

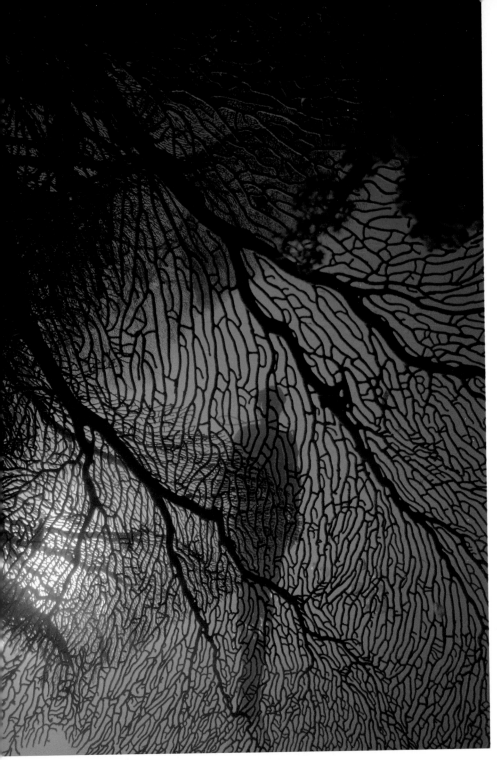

Giant sea fans at Ras Um Sid frame an ascending diver.

possible to make diving arrangements on the spot, reservations are recommended then as well. The live-aboard boats, which generally dock at Sharm El Sheikh, travel throughout the area. Reservations for them should always be made in advance.

The sites of Naama Bay are among the most heavily dived in the Red Sea. Yet, as a result of the dive guides' efforts to enforce the spearfishing ban and prohibit the taking of marine life, the reefs are in excellent condition. Some of the diving is done from beaches, with walks of about 50 yards or less over fringing coral reefs (or swims at high tide) to reach the dropoffs.

RAS NASRANI marks the beginning of the Gulf of Aqaba and the Straits of Tiran. Located north of the Sharm El Sheikh airport at the end of an ambiguous dirt road, the site has a beautiful white sand beach. Dive guides often bring their groups here for two dives, with a beach and lunch break in between. Be sure to bring an extra water bottle and sunscreen.

The deeper side is to the north (left from the entry point), so that dive is usually made first. This area is often the site of strong currents which bring oceanic fish, especially in summer. That makes Ras Nasrani one of the best places in Sinai to observe pelagic creatures, providing the potential for high-energy excitement. Whale sharks have been seen here. Tuna and jacks, rays and turtles are common visitors, with mantas and sharks more likely in winter. A sloping gray wall drops into sand at 150 feet. Interspersed coral heads are covered with soft corals, lending large splashes of color to an otherwise monochromatic seascape. Some outcrops have as much as 25 feet of vertical relief, and are surrounded by goldfish and sweepers. A spectacular array of sea fans is stacked along the wall north of the entry, from 50 to over 120 feet deep. Individual fans, as large as 20 feet across, have soft corals growing on them. They provide an excellent foreground for wide angle photography. The deeper caves sometimes house sleeping sharks.

To the right of the entry is a shallow slope with reefs cut by sand channels. If you spend the day at Ras Nasrani, this will usually be the second dive. There are fewer soft corals and less color, but this is an excellent spot for closeup photography and for observing reef fish. The shallow reefs, at 15 feet and less, are honeycombed with small caves that house sweepers, soldierfish, and an occasional grouper. A couple of medium sized Napoleon Wrasses inhabit the area. In the sand at 60 feet lives a large colony of garden eels which can be approached closely if the diver is patient. Ras Nasrani is also an excellent area for night dives, with flashlight fish, crabs and Spanish Dancers.

FAR GARDEN can be reached only by boat. This is a sloping wall with a few coral outcrops where *Anthias* aggregate around coral formations and sea fans. Reef fish also concentrate around these formations, making this a good area for both closeup and wide-angle photography. Work the coral outcrops for fish closeups. There are also some interesting caves between 10 and 20 feet. The safe, easy anchorage makes Far Garden an excellent spot for night diving. You are almost certain to see Spanish Dancers.

THE CATHEDRAL, a deeper part of Far Garden, is for advanced divers only. The reef slopes to a depth of 130 feet where an overhang forms a deep cave. Whip corals and large white soft corals surround the arching entrance, making it seem like the doorway to a cathedral. The cave extends some 30 feet back into the reef, but the entrance can be seen at all times. Large moray eels inhabit the area, and interesting pelagics sometimes swim by.

The closest diving spot north of Naama Bay is NEAR GARDEN, a relaxed, low-key dive for all levels of ability. Its best features are the coral formations and sand-dwelling organisms which make it an excellent place for closeup photography. The reef table drops off to a sandy bottom at 10 feet, that gradually slopes to 130 feet. Small outcrops with fan and table corals dot the slope. Look beneath the corals for bottom-dwelling crocodile fish, stingrays, and starfish. Jacks, unicorn fish, and barracudas often swim by the point. A resident Napoleon cruises by divers, expecting a handout. Accessible from the beach or by boat, Near Garden offers views of nearly all Red Sea life. At the edge of the dropoff, in 80 or 90 feet, look for large black coral trees and even larger gorgonian fans. If diving from a boat, swim the dropoff in an easterly direction from the mooring.

Many divers ignore NAAMA BAY, but the beach area in front

of the dive centers offers easy access and interesting marine life. Because of the fine sand bottom, visibility here is usually limited to 40 feet and less. Shallow reefs at 15-20 feet offer closeups of reef fish, especially many calm and docile lionfishes. Beyond the reefs, a sea grass bed gradually slopes into deep water. Lionfish, tinted green to match their surroundings, often hover over holes in the sand seeking prey. Cassiopea jellyfish are common here, and even sea horses have been reported. A large turtle, hosting several remoras, is a permanent resident and can often be found in the sea grass. The uneven sandy bottom is marked with dunes and valleys and scattered reefs. Wreckage from a salvage barge and a large anchor can be found at about 90 feet. This is an excellent site for twilight and night dives. In the evening it can be an ethereal dive, as the soft sand bottom makes it seem as though the reefs are rising out of the mist.

THE TOWER gets its name from a rock formation above the beach entry point. Entry can be be made through a cut in the reef, which opens to the rugged topography of a vast coral canyon. The sheer wall drops straight down to 300 feet, interspersed with small coral formations that are decorated with soft corals and surrounded by goldfish. All the interesting life is concentrated around the coral heads at depths of 100 feet and less. Following the wall to the left (north), there are small caves and overhangs. Usually lacking big fish, this is a place for closeup photography and wide angle silhouettes. However, manta rays and sharks have occasionally been observed here. Because of the short walk over the fringing reef, this is also an excellent site for night diving. Flashlight fish are common in the caves; octopus and cuttlefish may also be observed. Look into small crevices in coral heads for hundreds of sleeping *Anthias.*

PARADISE is one of the best places to see striking coral formations. Entry is down a rocky trail, then 50 yards over the reeftop. The sloping wall is interspersed with fantastic shapes of large pillars and towers. Many are topped by table corals, gorgonians, and soft corals. There are all kinds of natural arches and lattice work for dramatic silhouettes. Some house schools of silver sweepers. The largest formations seem like old, dead things with

Pinky's Wall is one of the best locations in Sinai for rich soft corals.

new growth on top of them. Most of the interesting ones lie at depths from 60 to 80 feet. The further south one goes, the more varied shapes are encountered. Soft corals lend a touch of color, but aside from an occasional moray eel and curious Napoleon fish, small reef fish predominate. This is also an excellent spot for night diving.

PINKY'S WALL is a classic wall dive. Entry is a hike down a rocky ravine, then a short walk over the reef table. The sheer drop continues a long way down, but the best scenery is around the 50 to 70 foot level, and gets better as you proceed further south. Crevices and overhangs are decorated with spectacular soft corals, some of them growing over old strands of fishing line. This is one of the best spots in Sinai for profuse, uninterrupted soft corals. Perhaps because of the recessed location of the wall, there are few big fish, but lots of *Anthias* and sweepers hover around the outcrops. Sometimes divers will enter at Pinky's, swim south along the wall, and exit at Amphoras.

The remains of an ancient shipwreck give AMPHORAS its name. About a half dozen small amphoras, overgrown with some eight hundred years of corals, are scattered around the reef at the 75 to 80 foot levels. The remains of three or four larger ones are there as well, along with an old anchor. Unfortunately, the largest amphoras were taken from the site a couple of years ago. Some of the jars contained mercury. Look for blackened areas on the corals, then fan the sand below to find the silvery liquid. There are many large coral formations, similar to Paradise.

FIASCO REEF got its name from a dive when everything that could go wrong did, and the guides never forgot it. Like many dive sites in the area, the barren wall slopes gradually, with large coral heads scattered from 50 to 65 feet. There are nice table corals with sea fans and small schools of sweepers. The coral formations display wonderfully strange shapes, similar to those at Paradise. They are full of reef fish, nudibranchs, moray eels with cleaner shrimp, and blue spotted stingrays. Watch the outside waters for an occasional turtle.

Around the corner from Fiasco, RAS UM SID is the favorite spot of many Sinai dive guides. A point rising up out of deep water,

The Shark Observatory marks the southernmost end of Ras Muhammed Wall.

it attracts numerous pelagic creatures. Therefore the diver should divide his attention between the reef and open water. This is one of the few places to observe manta rays in the summer months, especially when there is a lot of plankton in the water. Tuna are also frequent summer visitors; sharks and turtles can be seen throughout the year. A military checkpoint is located on the bluff overlooking the dive site. Entry is a 40-yard walk over a fringing coral reef, or you can snorkel it at high tide. A hole in the top of the reef exits through a cave at 15 feet. The wall drops straight to a 100-foot plateau, then slopes more gradually beyond diving depth. The best diving is between 50 and 80 feet. Go north (left) from the entry, swimming toward the point. There will be strong currents during tidal changes, but that brings in the big fish. A spectacular array of sea fans is stacked the wall beginning shallow and continuing over 120 feet, feeding on plankton brought in by the current. This is a place where a careful observer can spot a tremendous variety of fish and invertebrates. Schools of barracuda, snappers and surgeonfish swim by the wall. The coral heads, generally small but abundant, are covered with colorful soft corals, surrounded by goldfish and other reef creatures. Look in the crevices for scorpionfish, morays, and black lionfish. Torpedo rays, crocodile fish, and blue-spotted stingrays hide in the sand patches. A large Napoleon, Sid, has been fed by the dive guides and usually cruises around checking out new visitors. This is an especially exciting twilight dive, with frantic fish activity. It is also an excellent night dive at high tide, when you can snorkel over the shallow fringing reef to avoid sea urchins.

THE TEMPLE is a long swim from the beach, so it's usually dived from a boat. Two coral columns rise from the sand at 50 feet, the larger one almost reaching the surface. It is split by a crevice, with sea fans and soft corals growing in the cleft, a school of sweepers spilling around the scene. Several smaller pinnacles surround the columns. The lush growth, the colors, and the reef fish make this a beautiful background for wide-angle photography. A significant portion of the book *Samantha* was filmed here. With its clear, shallow water and no currents, this is an excellent spot for novice divers. Resident reef creatures include angelfish, parrotfish, butterfly fish, puffers, triggerfish and lionfish. Large Napoleons sometimes cruise by. This is also an excellent night dive. You are likely to see Spanish Dancers, shrimp, hermit crabs, and an occasional cuttlefish. Look in the small crevices for sleeping parrotfish, and in the larger caves for a sleeping Napoleon.

RAS MUHAMMED

Dr. Eugenie Clark once stated that if she could dive only one place in the world it would be Ras Muhammed. That statement isn't as restrictive as it sounds, because Ras Muhammed isn't one dive, it's about a dozen. Located some 20 miles by dirt road from Naama Bay, the tip of the peninsula offers some of the most spectacular diving found anywhere in the world. It can be reached by car or boat from Naama Bay, or on an overnight boat trip from Hurghada. Therefore, divers based at either Sharm El Sheikh or Hurghada have the opportunity to make these dives. Ras Muhammed will keep divers enchanted and enthused not only for the duration of a trip, but as long as the stories of their experiences there are retold.

At the time this was written, the entire MARSA BAREKA area was off limits to diving for reasons of military security. Check at the dive center for current regulations regarding this region.

MARSA BAREKA is a large bay just north of Ras Muhammed, offering an excellent anchorage for overnight boats, especially in bad weather. On the northern shore is a 50-foot sand dune, ending at the water's edge. A boat can run its keel into the sand, then discharge its passengers for a beach interlude. The view from the top of the dune is spectacular, and it's fun to run or roll down the sand into the water.

Diving near the north end of Marsa Bareka is marginal, because sand flows have killed most of the corals. The best dive site is its southern point, RAS ATAR. Beginning at the surface, the fringing reef drops off in a sheer wall with caves and overhangs. Table corals project horizontally from the wall. Large schools of barracuda and snappers can be observed swimming by. Due to strong currents, this is usually a drift dive.

RAS ATIK (Lion's Head) gets its name from a large rock formation on the cliff above the dive site. It is a drift dive by boat, or a beach dive with a short swim from the south end of Marsa Bareka. A large cave with a steeply arched opening is filled with silver sweepers. Called Yatza Cave after the founder of the Israeli Dive Federation, it is a favorite of underwater photographers. The arch provides a dramatic frame for diver silhouettes. (Remember, the above sites may still be off limits to divers.)

RAS MUHAMMED WALL extends from the eel garden in the north to the Shark Observatory in the south, a distance of nearly a half kilometer. Above the surface is a sheer limestone cliff with a fringing reef below. Its southern end is a large rock formation called the Shark Observatory. The Israelis built a stairway and a railing from which to watch schooling fish below. Directly beneath it is the sheerest and deepest part of the wall.

This spot is for advanced divers only. There is no place for a boat to anchor and it's too long a swim from the beach, so it can only be done as a drift dive. Prevailing northerly winds usually make it choppy near the wall. Therefore, the boat will drop and pick up divers about 30 yards away. The wall is too long and there is too much to see for just one dive. Maximum depths range from

80 feet to over 300. Although the scenery at 30 to 60 feet is the most colorful and spectacular, the temptation is always there to go deeper. Watch your depth and bottom time.

Calling Ras Muhammed a wall dive is like calling the Mona Lisa a painting. It's the masterpiece of wall dives. Drifting southward with the gentle current, every ledge and crevice has something different to catch your eye and dazzle your mind. Colorful soft corals grow from overhangs, surrounded by *Anthias*, which flutter around the wall like butterflies. Giant gorgonian fans, up to 15 feet across, spread horizontally on some of the ledges. A few areas, especially in deep cevices, are dark and comparatively devoid of life.

Brillantly colored soft corals dominate the outcrops along the walls at Ras Muhammed.

Others are brilliantly colorful and alive with activity. Caves provide refuge for soldierfish, hatchetfish, and silver sweepers. Points and outcrops can be rainbows of brilliant colors. The perceptive diver will remember to look occasionally toward open water. Facing into the deepest waters of the Red Sea, the wall of Ras Muhammed attracts pelagic species in search of prey. Schools of jacks or tuna, or perhaps a shark or an eagle ray, may swim by. At the north end, an 80-foot sand plateau is virtually covered with garden eels. To the south, underneath the Shark Observatory, the sheerest wall drops straight down well beyond diving depth. At 100 feet on a clear day, you can look up and see the surf breaking on top of the reef. Looking down, the vibrant colors fade into the indigo blue of infinity. The feeling is one of awe and insignificance, like standing on a mountaintop and realizing how small you are.

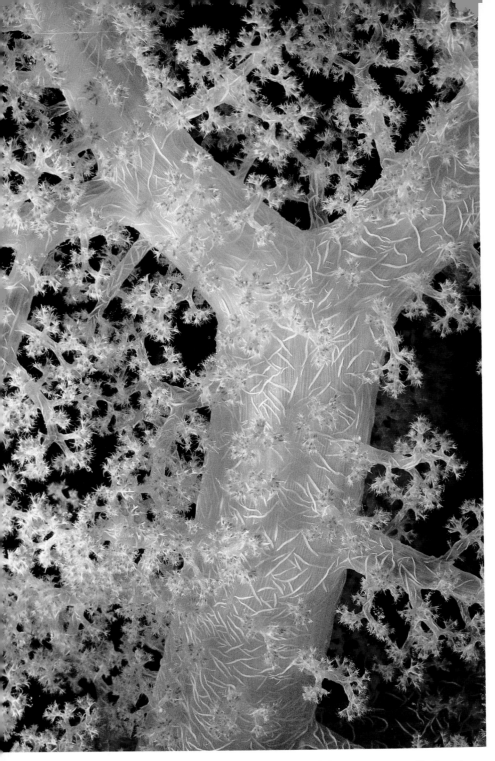

A photographer's delight, soft corals, Dendronephthya *sp., are usually found in areas of strong current.*

DIVING WITH COMPUTERS

Decompression computers are having a profound impact on diving practices, because multi-level diving can now be plotted accurately, resulting in significantly longer bottom times. Many Red Sea dive guides use them, and most operators allow divers to rely on these instruments instead of the tables. But because a computer is merely an alogorithm of the tables, and cannot sense the user's physiology or exertion rate, certain precautions are necessary. Don't push your dive profile to the limits. Either ascend to shallower water before the meter calls for decompression, or save enough air to spend more than the required time at the decompression stops. Users call this the "fudge factor".

Slower ascent rates are essential for preventing bubble formation. The American Academy of Underwater Sciences recommends a rate of 30 feet per minute from 60 feet to the surface. Makers of some computers require rates as slow as 20 feet per minute.

AAUS also recommends a five-minute safety stop between 10 and 30 feet for any dive. (If decompression is required, this should be added to the schedule.) This is a simple, yet effective means of avoiding silent bubble formation. It also helps control the ascent rate and allows you to listen for motors overhead.

In the Red Sea, decompression is sometimes necessary to realize the full potential of diving opportunities. But toss aside visions of long, cold, boring stops on an anchor line. Since most reefs and walls begin at the surface, decompression is not an onerous task. You can do it while watching colorful fish and coral scenery in shallow water, an enjoyable epilogue to your dive.

Since SHARK REEF is more easily accessible by land and by boat, far more diving is done there than on Ras Muhammed Wall. By land it's an hour drive over dirt roads from Naama Bay to the tip of the peninsula. There are mooring buoys at the south end of the reef for dive boats.

If we were to pick one dive in Sinai on which you could see the greatest variety of Red Sea fish, this is it. Dive guides have been feeding the reef fish, so they gather around the mooring as soon as they hear the boat's propeller. It's like an underwater petting zoo, as Napoleons, parrotfish, and triggerfish compete for handouts. On the deep side, vast schools of pelagics patrol the deeper outside water looking for prey. Looking upward, a huge aggregation of jacks, batfish, unicorn fish, or barracuda, can darken the surface like a living cloud. On one dive, Mia pointed frantically off into the distance. I wondered what she was so excited about, because it looked like just another reef. Upon approaching more closely I realized it wasn't a reef at all, but a dense, living ball of large snappers. As I entered the school and looked down, the fish parted to reveal two whitetip sharks and a large hammerhead hovering below.

This is one of the best places in Sinai to observe sharks. Hammerheads are common from May to October, as are oceanic whitetips. Winter is the mating season for sharks; grays, whitetips and blacktips are likely to be encountered.

The current at Shark Reef usually flows in a southerly direction, and can be quite strong during tidal changes. When it really rips, you may have to pull yourself along the bottom and rest in crevices. At those times, it's not a place for novice divers. But that's what attracts all the oceanic fish.

It is best to dive the reef in a clockwise direction. That way, you will have to fight the current for only a third of the dive. Proceed north from the anchorage along a sandy bottom interspersed with coral heads. From 30 feet, a sand canyon slopes into deep water. To the left, at about 90 feet, is a group of large sea fans. Follow the wall opposite the sea fans around to the right, where small crevices afford protection when the current is really strong. There are caves, overhangs and sea fans like Ras Muhammed

The stonefish sheds its skin when it becomes too overgrown with the marine life that aids its camouflage. This one is a resident of the shallow area at Shark Reef.

Wall, except everything is more concentrated. Some divers like to leave the wall and swim among the schools of pelagic fish in blue water. Be especially careful of your depth, because in blue water you could be descending without realizing it. And set a compass heading to return to the reef.

After circumnavigating the reef, you will finish back on the sandy bottom. This is a beautiful spot to observe reef fishes. Black surgeonfish and Napoleons hang out here expecting to be fed by divers. At least two stonefish are permanent residents. Use the shallow area near the mooring buoy for decompression if necessary.

JOLANDA REEF is located just south of Shark Reef. A South African freighter, the *Jolanda* hit this reef and sank in 1981. For five years it provided a spectacular setting for underwater photographers. However, a violent storm in early 1987 sent it over the edge into more than 300 feet of water. Wreckage from the ship — including cargo containers filled with sinks and toilet bowls — still lies strewn about the reef. Sand patches are home to large trigger-

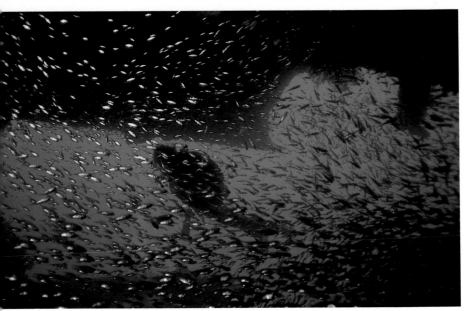

Silver sweepers fill the hull of the Dunraven, *a 100 year old British merchant vessel.*

fish, which can be seen protecting their nests in summer. The multicolored Titan triggerfish is common here. Schools of unicorn fish and batfish commonly move between the two reefs.

The outside edge of this reef is another wall dive, a mini version of Shark Reef. Proceed in a clockwise direction around the reef. The wall drops to a sand plateau with small coral heads at 80 feet, then continues to slope deeper. Whip corals and violet gorgonians grow from the slope. Watch the open water for big pelagic fish. Tuna are common in summer. Schools of unicorn fish and other surgeonfish species hang out closer to the wall. Finish the dive at 20 feet, where you can observe reef fish in and around the shallow caves.

Around the corner from Ras Muhammed is an area protected by a fringing reef which makes an excellent night anchorage. Boat skippers call the area ALTERNATIVE REEFS, because it is diveable when severe wind and weather conditions prevent a dive at Ras Muhammed. It's a good site in its own right, especially at night. There are about 15 coral heads rising from a sandy bottom,

30 feet deep inside, sloping gently to 70 feet outside. The reefs run in an east-west direction, with the best diving on the outside edge. A crevice at 40 feet is completely filled with a huge black coral tree. During the day you are likely to see turtles, rays, and perhaps a nurse shark resting in the sand. At night lobsters are common in the shallows, especially on top of the reefs. Crevices house sleeping parrotfish and masked puffers, while giant puffers roam around the reef. Like pigeons on a rooftop, a remarkable variety of crinoids perch atop the coral heads at night.

Northward into the Gulf of Suez, the wreck of the *Dunraven* lies in 90 feet of water at the foot of BEACON ROCK. The most famous wreck in the Red Sea, it was discovered by some Israeli divers in the mid 1970's. At first they thought it was a ship used by Lawrence of Arabia to finance his campaign against the Turks during World War I. Later research showed it to be a merchant ship that caught fire and sank around 1880. At first glance the wreck is a bit of a disappointment. Covered with 100 years' growth and broken apart near the bow, it really doesn't look much like a ship any more. However, it is possible to swim through the hull. Enough light penetrates the broken plates to avoid the claustrophobic feeling one would get in a completely dark ship-wreck, but be sure to bring a flashlight to see details. A ship's wheel, probably not the original, is a great prop for photographs. But don't get any ideas about taking it. The dive guides make sure that all remaining artifacts are left for others to enjoy.

Visibility on the *Dunraven* is usually poor by Red Sea standards, due to lots of suspended matter. The best photo spot is the entrance to the stern section, where a diver can be silhouetted by the wreckage and a huge school of silver sweepers.

DIVING ITINERARY FOR SINAI

All diving itineraries are dependent upon weather and, when land-based, upon boat schedules. If you go with a dive center for five days to a week, they will see to it that you have the opportunity to visit the best sites in the area. It won't necessarily be in the order given here but should include the places mentioned.

CAIRO DIVERS

Anyone diving for any length of time in the Red Sea is likely to run into a member of Cairo Divers. Egypt's leading dive club, they number over 300 strong. Members come from all walks of life, from doctors to laborers, and from many different nationalities. About a fourth of them are Egyptian; the others are a United Nations of expatriates working or living in Egypt. Like any dive club around the world they share one thing: a love of the undersea environment. Club dives are organized on a regular basis to various Red Sea diving sites. Instruction is offered at many levels, from Basic Scuba through Divemaster. Since many of the regulars have been diving Sinai and Hurghada for years, they not only know the more familiar areas but have also visited some of the exotic locations in the South. Members of Cairo Divers have been to The Brothers, Zhabarghad Island, Port Sudan, and beyond. If you are seeking information or help for a trip there, it could be worthwhile to contact someone in the club.

Meetings are held the first Monday of each month at a downtown hotel. Officers are subject to change, so the best way to get in touch with them is to get a current address from one of the dive centers. Another possibility is to contact the American Embassy in Cairo. It's nice to communicate with people who know the country and its diving scene. Most members are more than willing to help visiting divers. Language and cultural differences are bridged by a common interest in diving.

LAND-BASED: All the centers at Naama Bay have access to boats, but not every day, especially during high season. Many sites are more convenient to dive from the beach due to the lack of an adequate anchorage for large boats.

Here is a sample itinerary:
Day one: Far Garden and The Temple
Day two: Ras Nasrani and The Tower, night dive at Naama Bay
Day three: Straits of Tiran
Day four: Pinky's Wall and Paradise
Day five: Shark Reef and Ras Muhammed Wall
Day six: Amphoras and Ras um Sid, night dive at The Tower
Day seven: Repeat Shark Reef & Ras Muhammed

If additional days are available, the diving can be broken up with a two-day trip by car to St. Catherine's Monastery. On the way you can stop at Dahab and dive any of its sites through that dive center.

SHIP-BASED: A live-aboard boat will usually offer four daily dives, the last at night. The night dive will usually be made at the anchorage for the evening. Depending on the ship's schedule, there are three circular routes available: the Tiran Islands, Ras Muhammed area, and the Straits of Gubal. A sample itinerary follows:
Day one: The Temple, Ras Um Sid, The Temple (night)
Day two: Tiran Island: Rock point and Pinnacles, Kush Kashkar (night)
Day three: Jackson Reef, Thomas Reef, Gordon Reef
Day four: Ras um Sid, Pinky's Wall, Ras um Sid (night)
Day five: Shark Reef, Ras Muhammed Wall, Alternatives (night)
Day six: Shag Rock, Dunraven, Alternatives (night)
Day seven: Ras Muhammed Wall, Shark Reef

Someone staying on a boat an additional week could dive the sites in the Straits of Gubal (see next chapter), or perhaps more of the mainland Sinai sites, or repeat the Ras Muhammed area.

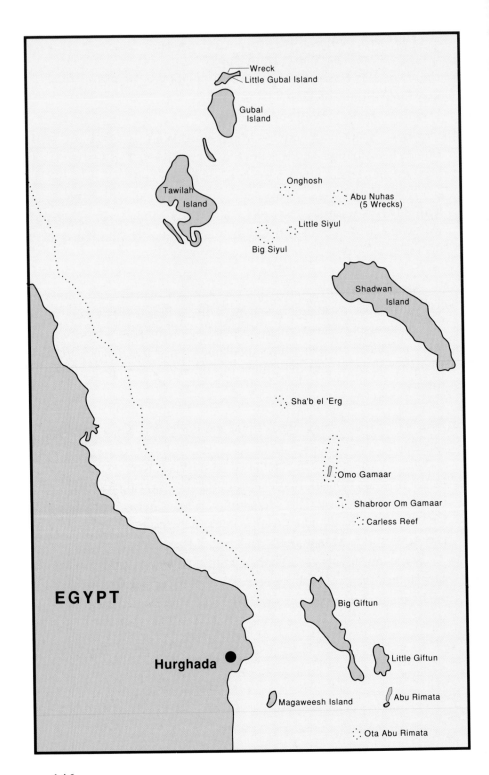

Wreck
Little Gubal Island

Gubal
Island

Onghosh

Abu Nuhas
(5 Wrecks)

Tawilah
Island

Little Siyul

Big Siyul

Shadwan
Island

Sha'b el 'Erg

Omo Gamaar

Shabroor Om Gamaar

Carless Reef

EGYPT

Big Giftun

Little Giftun

Hurghada

Magaweesh Island

Abu Rimata

Ota Abu Rimata

146

Chapter 6

Hurghada

Hurghada was originally a fishing village and military base on the Red Sea coast, located 235 miles south of Suez. Diving tourism in the Red Sea began there in the mid 1960s when Peter and Helga Kopp set up the first dive operation. They developed a loyal European clientele and explored many of the sites described here.

A marine laboratory was established at Hurghada in 1930 by the British. Eugenie Clark did her initial research in the Red Sea there in 1951 with Dr. H.A.F. Gohar, Egypt's most renowned marine biologist. She wrote about it in her first book, *Lady with a Spear*. The laboratory is still in operation, along with a small museum and aquarium which are open to the public.

Today, hotels in Hurghada cater to a variety of tastes and budgets, ranging from international class to hostel style. Many Egyptian families come here in summer to escape Cairo. Nightlife is limited to the large hotel bars and shopping is confined to the essentials. However, beach resorts offer sailboarding, fishing trips, water skiing, and snorkeling excursions for non-divers. European divers predominate, particularly Germans, who can take advantage of direct charter flights. Advance reservations are recommended especially in winter, but during most of the year you can arrive un-

Hurghada is the primary fishing port on the Red Sea, and home to a colorful fleet.

announced and make arrangements on the spot with one of the many dive centers.

In the past, most Hurghada dive centers used rented fishing boats for diving trips. Although seaworthy, these boats were slow, noisy, and uncomfortable. Today most operators have their own boats, built expressedly for diving. These vessels are 50 to 60 feet long, powered by diesel engines, with far more room and comfort than the fishing boats. Their construction marked a major step in the development of Hurghada dive operations.

From Cairo, daily Egypt Air flights to Hurghada take less than an hour. However, they are in heavy demand and should be booked well in advance. Service is also available from Sharm el Sheikh and Luxor to Hurghada. Check airline schedules for the most current information, because there are plans to add more flights.

Air-conditioned buses make the trip from Cairo in eight to ten hours. It is easier and cheaper to obtain space on the buses than on airplanes, and one of them travels overnight. A third option is to hire a car, which can make the journey in about six hours.

Many of the Hurghada dive sites are patch reefs, rising from mid water.

A visit to Luxor and the Valley of the Kings can easily be combined with a diving trip to Hurghada. Two days is enough time for the casual visitor to see the temples and tombs, although the serious archaeology buff will want to stay longer. A hired car can make the journey from Hurghada in three and a half hours.

Most dive sites in the Hurghada area are small islands or reefs rising from the deep. Therefore most of the diving is from boats. The reefs look like sunken islands, with the coral heads exposed only at low tide. From a distance, they appear as turquoise patches on a sapphire blue sea. The area can be subdivided into three sections: The Strait of Gubal, Hurghada and Safaga.

THE STRAIT OF GUBAL

These sites lie three hours or more north of the port of Hurghada. They are usually dived on overnight trips, using Little Gubal Island or Shadwan Island as a base.

SHA'AB ALI is a large reef area off the western coast of Sinai. Although oil drilling has been going on there for several years, the water is clean and the reef has good potential for diving, but prevailing currents can cause difficulties. There are three large wrecks on the main reef, all visited regularly by fishermen. One of them lies on a slope, from 30 feet to 80 feet. A large reserve propeller is on the upper deck, so shallow that you can see it snorkeling. Table corals cover many of the metal parts. The second wreck, about 60 years old, is broken up. Little is known about the third.

One spot visited fairly regularly by boats from Sharm El Sheikh and from Hurghada is SHAG ROCK, at the southern end of Sha'ab Ali. Although most of the reef is submerged, the rocky area above the surface is frequented by cormorants, known locally as shags. The reef itself is some 500 yards long by 100 yards wide. A steep wall drops to a sandy shelf at 80 feet. Along its face are several small, well-hidden caves. Inside, nurse and whitetip sharks often sleep by day before roaming the reef to feed at night. Sometimes they lie on top of one another inside the caves. Look on the sandy shelf for guitar sharks, nurse sharks, leopard sharks and an occasional turtle. Due to the current, this is often a drift dive.

The venomous lionfish can be approached very closely by a careful diver.

On the northern end of the reef, about 30 feet deep, lies a wreck, perhaps a hundred years old. Only the framework of the stern section remains, but it makes a good background for photographs. Big moray eels and many table corals can be seen around the wreck. It is diveable only when the northerly winds aren't blowing.

SHADWAN, the largest island in the Strait of Gubal, is seldom dived. Due to its strategic location in the mouth of the Gulf of Suez, it was a military outpost during the wars with Israel. Soldiers stationed there lobbed an occasional grenade over the edge, causing considerable damage to the reefs. The island itself still contains land mines, so camping is prohibited. Today Shadwan is sometimes used as an anchorage from which to make overnight trips to other areas including Gubal Island, Abu Nuhas, and Sinai. Although Shadwan is about fifteen miles long, the difficulty of anchoring on the outside restricts the diving area. When the north wind isn't blowing, the outside has lots of potential. A sheer wall drops into very deep water; oceanic sharks are frequent visitors. The middle third of the island is one of the best places in the Red Sea to observe large sharks, including threshers, hammerheads, tigers, whitetips, and blacktips. Schools of barracuda, large tuna, and other pelagic fish can be seen swimming by. Sport fishermen often go there in search of marlin and sailfish.

Most of the inside is shallow, sandy area providing marginal diving. One exception is the southern end, around the corner from the lighthouse, where vast schools of jacks congregate in June and July. Shadwan is the subject of legend and superstition among the local fishermen who consider it a jinxed island. But the main reason it isn't dived more is that better and easier diving can be found much closer to Sinai and Hurghada.

Off the northwest end of Shadwan is a small reef called SHABROOR SIYUL. Small coral heads rise from the sand in shallow water at the southern end of the reef. Tuna, jacks and barracuda often swim by in open water; Napoleon wrasses frequent the area. Nurse and whitetip sharks can often be seen sleeping under the table corals. This spot usually has a strong current flowing northward.

Looking dark and foreboding, Abu Nuhas is a graveyard for five shipwrecks.

SIYUL KABIRAH, or Big Siyul, is located northwest of Shabroor Siyul. Part of the reef can be seen above the surface. On the northwest side, about 20 feet deep, are some nice caves containing soft corals and sweepers. Black coral can also be seen in the shallow water. The eastern side drops off to a shelf at 50 feet, then slopes to 70. Sometimes nurse sharks can be spotted sleeping in the sand.

SHA'AB UM 'USH, or Onghosh Reef, is usually a second site after diving Shadwan or en route to Gubal Island. Scenery consists primarily of coral outcrops with the usual mix of reef fish. A wall slopes to 100 feet, but the best diving is around the 40 to 60 foot mark.

ABU NUHAS has been called the greatest navigation hazard in the northern Red Sea. It is also a wreck diver's dream come true. Four large freighters have run aground there, two of them protruding partially out of the water. All of them lie on the unprotected northwest end of the reef, so this is a drift dive in all but the calmest seas. The four most accessible wrecks are known by their cargoes. The oldest, which hit the reef about 20 years ago, gave the reef its name. It carried a load of copper, Nuhas in Arabic. The Tile Wreck carried ceramic tiles, made in Spain, which have been damaged by the water and are not considered salvageable. The cargo of the Lentil Wreck was eaten by parrotfish and groupers. It has the most fish life of the four; perhaps the bonanza of free food kept schools of snappers and batfish hovering around. The most recent wreck, the *Giannis D.* — carrying hardwood from Greece — hit the reef in 1983 and remained stranded above water for six weeks until heavy waves caused it to break up and sink.

Recently a fifth shipwreck was discovered on Abu Nuhas by some Egyptian dive guides. Lying in 70 feet of water, it was a luxury liner, from 70 to 100 years old. Bottles still containing wine have been recovered which, unfortunately, had turned to vinegar. A family of Napoleon Wrasses frequents the wreck, along with many lionfish.

The same conditions which made Abu Nuhas the best wreck diving site in the Egyptian Red Sea combine to make it a difficult dive. Heavy wind chop and strong currents are usually encountered on the surface. Sand is stirred up on the shallow part of the reef, reducing visibility below the expected norm for this region. And perhaps because of fuel leakage, there is little invertebrate growth on the wrecks; they are relatively barren.

LITTLE GUBAL ISLAND, like Shadwan, is a base used by Hurghada dive centers for trips to Sinai. Unlike Shadwan, however, it offers a good campsite and four easily accessible dive areas. It is also the site of one of the first oil wells in the Middle East. There had been a sulfur mine on this desert island, but the hole kept filling up with oil, so the British began a small drilling operation in 1914. The rusting remains of the well and a couple of steam engines are still there on the plateau overlooking the campsite. Protected by a shallow coral reef, the bay on Little Gubal provides a fine anchorage for small boats. The white sand beach is an excellent campsite, but bring plenty of fresh water because none is available on the island. A sandspit between Little Gubal and Big Gubal Island is an interesting spot for tidepooling; the few shrubs nearby provide nesting space for seabirds. The reef, about 30 feet maximum depth, is a good beach dive with rich hard and soft corals and a large variety of reef fish. It's also a good place for a night dive.

The remains of a small barge lie in 40 feet of water at the northern end of the bay. Most of the deck is gone, but the hull and skeleton are covered with colorful soft corals, making it an excellent photo spot. Silver sweepers swarm around the ribs, while large spotted groupers can be seen hiding in crevices. The reef table around the wreck is alive with hard and soft corals and the usual mixture of reef fish. At night, crinoids, basket stars, and nocturnal crabs make it an interesting dive.

An unmanned light marks the northwestern point of the island. Directly below it on the northern side is a sloping wall, dropping off to over 130 feet. Pelagic fish often swim by; schools of jacks are common visitors. Sharks can often be observed at twilight, attracted by the feeding behavior of the reef fish. At night, parrotfish sleep in caves and crevices and flashlight fish blink their lights among the crinoids and basket stars. Strong currents are common during tidal changes, usually running southward, so a good prac-

Large groupers surround the deep wreck on the north end of Little Gubal Island.

tice is to have a boat standing by to pick up divers.

A fringing reef extends along the northern shore of Little Gubal, open to the full fury of the winds funneling out of the Gulf of Suez. Nearly a hundred years ago, a large freighter hit the reef and sank on its slope. The bow sits on top of the slope in six feet of water; the stern is 80 feet down. Its cargo consisted of ceramic insulators and old batteries, many of which can still be found inside. The hull has been split open so it is relatively easy for divers to penetrate the wreck. Groupers in the 25-pound class live inside, along with sweepers, goldfish, angelfish, and soft corals. Several larger groupers and Napoleons, weighing well over 200 pounds, frequent the deeper section. There is no anchorage on the northern shore of the island, so this is always a drift dive.

A large oil spill occurred in the Gulf of Suez in the spring of 1982. Prevailing winds deposited some of the mess on the northern beaches of Little Gubal Island. Fortunately, the reefs did not appear to be affected. During the first summer, globules of crude oil were still floating on the surface, even on the lee side. The next year they had sunk into the sand, but bathers still occasionally stepped on them. Three years later, the sea had finally cleansed itself, but the oil-fouled northern shore still bore mute witness to an ecological debacle.

HURGHADA AND VICINITY

The Hurghada area includes all dive sites located within two hours from the port, which can be reached on a day trip. When heavy winds are blowing out of the north, the boats will generally head south of town for the day's diving. When winds are light or absent, they head north.

TAWILA ISLAND, south of Gubal Island, isn't dived much because it is surrounded by shallow water. Several large saltwater pools are found inland, away from the beach. Tidepool fish swim in the extremely warm water and sea grass grows on the bottom. Just south of the island lies a reef, SHA'AB TAWILA, which is sometimes dived on the way to Gubal. Guitar sharks and large black stingrays lie on the sandy bottom at 40 feet. Look closely,

Schools of tuna cruise along a wall, seemingly oblivious to the divers' presence.

156

FISH FEEDING

Baksheesh is the Arabic term for a monetary handout or a tip. Fish respond well to baksheesh, and will become your friend at least as long as the food holds out. Offering food is one of the best ways to observe them at close quarters.

Some fish will eat anything, including leftover bread or hardboiled eggs. Others are more particular and insist upon fish. Either way, there are certain techniques which will bring in the maximum number of fish on a minimum of food, and keep them around for awhile. The most important concept is that less is better. Too much food will bring in a quick, frenzied herd which will depart as soon as you run out of baksheesh. Even a slice of bread can cloud the water in the immediate vicinity. The equivalent of a bite or two will entice almost as many fish, and keep them around looking for more. Other fish will quickly move in to see what all the excitement is about.

It is best to put the food in a tightly sealed plastic bag, and keep it hidden in a pocket or under your BC. Fish are smarter than you think. If you display the bag they will nip at it until it tears open, then attack the contents. Big fish have been known to swallow the entire bag. The diver should be in charge, not the fish. Open the bag carefully, taking out a small bit of food. Hold it in a tightly clenched fist; quickly reseal the bag and hide it. Then break off a small piece of food in the other hand and offer it to the fish. Tease them a little to keep them around, but if they act aggressive, let them have it. Triggerfish and others will nip a finger if they become too frustrated. Gloves are recommended.

Moray eels and big groupers sometimes act as if they were nearsighted. Overconfident divers have been bitten trying to feed these beasts. It is best to flip the food to them rather than letting them eat out of your hand. That's also good practice to follow with the smaller fish, until you get to know which ones you can trust.

On the reef, try leaving a small piece of food on a rock or a coral head, then watch as the fish moves in and examines it before taking it. Many underwater photographers use this technique to get closeup pictures. But watch out. Sometimes an aggressive wrasse will swoop in and steal the morsel you had set out to entice a shy moray eel.

FISH FEEDING (con't)

When working with a photographer, fish feeding is usually the job of the assistant. The goal is to manipulate the fish between the model and the camera. This allows the photographer to spotlight the fish in the picture, rather than the diver.

In areas where the fish are used to being fed, you can entice them even if you don't have food. At Shabroor Um Gamaar, a 300-pound Napoleon Wrasse (with a deformed mouth) arrives as soon as he hears divers' bubbles. By holding out a hand as if offering food, I was able to bring him in for an underwater ballet. He swam with me for ten minutes, allowing me to stroke the entire length of his five foot body and even to grab his tail. It finally ended when I had used up my bottom time. He followed me all the way into shallow water, wondering when he would receive baksheesh for the performance. I felt guilty for not having any to offer.

because they are often covered with sand and don't move unless you nearly land on them. Bigschools of jacks swim overhead, possibly because this area is rarely fished.

UMM GAMAAR, or Omo Gamaar, is a small islet with a fringing coral reef. An unmanned light is located on the north end, but the best diving is at the protected southern end. Many caves cut into the reef, several filled with schools of sweepers. On one dive, I continually had to bat the sweepers aside with my hand to make an opening large enough to silhouette the diver outside. On another occasion, a large blacktip shark was sleeping in a cave. The commotion of calling my buddy over to take a look apparently woke up the shark because, as we returned, it was staring at us from the mouth of the cave. A moment's hesitation cost me a sensational picture. Before I could get the camera ready, it quickly disappeared into open water with a powerful stroke of its tail. Obviously it was more startled and scared than we were.

At the midpoint of the island is a sloping wall, dropping off more than 140 feet. There is a very large cave at 80 feet, with lush soft corals growing around the entrance. Scattered coral heads

*At Omo Gamaar, the silver sweeper school parts to reveal a diver hovering
outside the mouth of a cave.*

159

along the wall provide shelter for puffers, soldierfish, and docile lionfish. Many coronetfish swim in the shallow water near the surface. This is one of the best places in the Red Sea to observe and photograph these curious animals. The shallow area has plenty of soft corals and reef fish activity, so one doesn't have to go deep to enjoy the dive. During January and February, manta rays often come here to mate. They can be observed feeding and carrying on courtship rituals.

South of Omo Gamaar lies one of the best dive sites in the area, the submerged reef, SHABROOR UM GAMAAR. It features a small shipwreck, tame groupers and Napoleons, and large schools of pelagic fish. Most of the action is centered around the wreck, said to be the remains of a torpedo boat, lying on the slope from 75 to 100 feet. The groupers, Charlie and Annie, usually appear as soon as they hear the boat's propeller and are waiting for the divers when they submerge. A pair of Napoleons usually follows; one of them has a deformed mouth. The groupers weigh around 150 pounds, the Napoleons probably twice that. Be careful when feeding the groupers because they have been known to get excited and nip a finger. The Napoleons, on the other hand, are extremely gentle. The one with the deformed mouth sometimes allows divers to stroke the entire length of its body. (See sidebar: Fish Feeding)

Many lionfish inhabit the shipwreck. They too are used to being fed, but that's best left to the dive guide because of the danger of inadvertently bumping their venomous spines.

Continuing along the wall beyond the wreck, look to outside water for a school of small tuna which frequents the area in summer. Schools of jacks, barracuda, and an occasional shark may also swim by. The best way to observe them is to get away from the other divers and swim along the wall at the 30 to 40 foot level, looking out and upward. Large schools of black surgeonfish always hover around the wall in summer. Egyptian fishermen call this behavior "farshad" (blanket) because the fish seem to cover the reefs like a blanket.

The shallow wall has many caves and crevices. At fifteen feet is a decompression cave where divers can make a leisurely stop while watching reef fish swim in and out. If you approached the limits of bottom time while playing with the groupers and Napole-

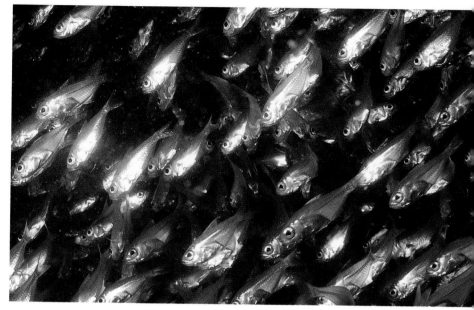

The bodies of silver sweepers, Parapriacanthus guentheri, *are partially transparent.*

ons, the cave is a convenient place to blow off excess nitrogen.

On all the charts it is called CARLESS REEF, but that could be a misspelling because everyone calls it Careless Reef. No one knows the reason for the name. Although a careless boat skipper could conceivably have run his vessel aground here, no shipwreck has yet been discovered. Perhaps the outstanding feature of this reef is its contingent of tame moray eels. Dive guide Ali Saad el Din has been feeding about a dozen morays over the last several years. He handles them to varying degrees. Some can be caressed and petted; one or two will wrap themselves around Ali and allow themselves to be cuddled. The problem is that only he knows which eel is which, and others have been bitten trying to cuddle the wrong animal. Therefore, feeding is best left to the dive guide.

The reef slopes to a wide plateau at 60 feet, then a wall drops off into deep water. A virtual forest of black coral trees begins at 80 feet and continues well past 150. Large gorgonian sea fans spread out horizontally in the current. Cruising sharks are common along the wall.

Napoleon wrasses, Cheilinus undulatus, *are the largest wrasses in the world, growing in excess of 400 pounds.*

The plateau has beautiful coral formations with soft corals and arches. Small caves are home for sweepers, bass, and even a small Napoleon. Fields of table corals provide shelter for sweetlips, bannerfish, butterflyfish, and spotted groupers. Goldfish swarm around the coral heads. Even without the moray eels, Carless Reef is an outstanding dive site.

During most of the year, SHA'AB AL IRQ, or El Erg, isn't anything special. But from January to March, the manta rays come in to feed and mate. The northern end of this horseshoe-shaped reef is the best spot in the Egyptian Red Sea to observe them. The water is rich in plankton at that time of year, so visibility may be down to about 50 feet.

A sand plateau at 40 feet is home for many garden eels that may sometimes be approached quite closely. Look for sleeping nurse sharks in the sand, and for reef fishes among the coral heads.

EL FANADIR is a long fringing reef running along the mainland north of Hurghada. In the past it was a place to observe sharks and large fish, but they were wiped out by spearfishermen in the

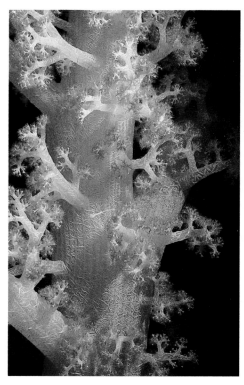

Dive guide Ali Saad El Din has tamed many of the morays at Carless Reef.

Found mostly in areas of current action, soft corals are a photographers delight.

70s, before that activity was banned. A sloping wall drops from the surface to about 140 feet, but the scenery is not exceptional. During January and February, however, turtles and eagle rays frequent the area.

EL BAREEMA, or The Lighthouse, is the closest dive spot to the town of Hurghada, a trip of less than a half hour in a fishing boat. Its shallow water and easy accessibility make it an excellent orientation dive for newcomers to the Red Sea. A coral reef west of Big Giftun Island, it barely reaches the surface, then drops off into sand at 40 feet. An automated light on the western end marks the anchorage and dive site. At first glance, this looks like a boring dive, but close observation will reveal many interesting reef creatures.

Two large coral heads dominate the sand bottom, with small patch reefs surrounding them. Look in the sand for small jellyfish, blennies sharing their burrow with commensal shrimp, conchs, and

163

blue-spotted stingrays. On the reefs look for lionfish, mapfish, big hermit crabs, and colorful soft corals. Moving into the patch reefs, you might spot a nurse shark in the sand or a school of barracuda overhead. Divers with patience and good powers of observation will rate this a serendipitous dive, much better than expected at first glance.

BIG GIFTUN ISLAND, facing Hurghada, isn't considered much of a dive site because it, too, is surrounded by shallow sandy bottom. But LITTLE GIFTUN, east of it, is another story. The best diving is on the southeastern (outside) end, where the wall drops to a sand plateau at 80 feet, then continues on a steep slope to 200 feet. Going over the edge, large outcrops with soft corals and black coral trees are observed as you continue down. A 200-pound grouper, which has been fed by local dive guides, often follows divers all the way to the bottom. Decompression is done on the shallow wall, where caves and crevices at 20 and 10 feet are alive with reef fish. Schools of unicorn fish and other surgeonfish swim by in the current.

Further north on the outside is another good deep dive. A sand

A hermit crab peers out from under its shell.

plateau interspersed with small coral heads slopes gently to 90 feet. The dropoff begins there, with many black coral trees. At 120 feet is a large cave with myriad soft corals inside. You enter through the top, then come out at 140 feet. A horizontal bar splits the upper opening into two parts, but it is wide enough for a diver to fit through easily.

On the southern point, a sand bottom at 55 feet is dotted with small coral heads. Groupers — in the 10 to 20 pound range — hover stationary over the sand, facing into the current. Many are being cleaned by small wrasses. Blue triggerfish stand guard over their nests in the summer. Surgeonfish schools cruise along the wall while parrotfish chew on the coral. This is a good shallow dive after a deep drop, with excellent opportunities to observe reef fish. There is some evidence of old dynamiting along the wall, with new coral growth beginning to heal the scars.

A large reef, called FANOOS, lies east of the island at about its midpoint. Giant sea fans face the current to the seaward side. A large cave at 80 feet has several black coral trees around the entrance. Big groupers are usually seen in this area, and dolphinfish sometimes cruise the outside water.

ABU RIMATA is a small, narrow islet with a fringing coral reef. The best diving is on the eastern side, which is exposed to wind chop. Anchoring can be difficult, so this is sometimes done as a drift dive. North of the islet, between it and Little Giftun, a wall begins at 60 feet and drops straight down to over 250 feet. There is a nice cave at 100 feet. Two tame groupers, Speedy and Gonzales, sometimes show up looking for handout. The prevailing current runs to the south, back toward Abu Rimata.

Another steep dropoff is found at the northern end of the islet, with an overhang near the surface. From 40 to 60 feet is a spectacular forest of giant sea fans, with individuals up to 15 feet across. Most of them spread horizontally from the wall. With small crinoids perched along their rims, they make excellent wide angle photographic subjects, especially with a diver to lend a sense of scale. Colorful soft corals among the sea fans make this one of the best wall dives in the Red Sea. Also look for a coral outcrop with a small cave inside, just big enough for one diver. Its soft

This coral grouper, Cephalopholis miniata, *is the main course of many delicious lunches on the Red Sea.*

corals provide a colorful frame for a photograph. Decompression is enhanced by excellent shallow scenery, including a large cave at 18 feet.

Near the southern end, two coral towers rise from the 50 foot sand bottom, almost reaching the surface. They are honeycombed with caves and grottoes containing a rich variety of multi-hued soft corals. An especially pretty grotto is at 30 feet, cutting through a corner of the reef. It is filled with soft corals, sweepers, and other reef fish. Black surgeonfish and parrotfish, along with schools of jacks, provide the fish activity. Near the surface, swarms of goldfish move back and forth with the surge. The tops of the reefs can be quite turbulent in heavy wind chop.

At the southern end, a sloping wall begins at 60 feet. Although the wall is mostly gray and colorless, a large coral formation at 100 feet has a beautiful central grotto with several openings leading in. Inside are soft corals, sweepers and soldierfish. A diver posing at one of the openings makes for good wide-angle photography. Below the grotto, at around 120 feet, are several large table coral

166

A cassiopea jellyfish hovers over a diver's gloved finger. It swims upside down, providing sunlight for the commensal algae growing in its tentacles.

formations. While decompressing along the wall, look for a large cave at 15 feet which is home to over a dozen lionfish.

At first glance, OTA ABU RIMATA doesn't look like much of a dive. The name means Pieces of Abu Rimata, but dive guides also call it THE AQUARIUM. The main reef barely reaches the surface, and many smaller coral heads surround it. Located about a half mile south of Abu Rimata, the reef drops off into sand at 40 feet. This may be the best place in the Egyptian Red Sea to observe schooling reef fish. Fish which are usually found singly or in pairs elsewhere congregate here in vast schools. Each school seems to stake out a territory, and as the diver proceeds counterclockwise from the anchorage on the eastern side of the reef, he will encounter one group of fish after another. We saw the bannerfish first, followed by spotted sweetlips, masked butterflyfish, then yellow grunts, and red snappers. Bigeye emperorfish, scarce in other locations, hang around the reefs in groups of three or four while being cleaned by tiny wrasses. Vast schools of jacks swim by fearlessly. Beyond the reef to the eastern side, look in the sand among the coral outcrops for crocodile fish, lionfish, and blue-spotted sting-rays. If you don't find them here, you won't find them anywhere. Triggerfish tend their nests in summer. Look in the sand for nurse sharks, and in the water overhead for schools of barracuda. Although this area is heavily dived, fish activity continues unabated. I once dove it with five dive boats anchored on the reef, and the fish didn't seem to mind. No one has explained the reasons for the schooling activity. It could be tied into feeding, mating, or cleaning.

MAGAWEESH ISLAND lies a couple of miles offshore from the resort of the same name. It is surrounded by shallow sand and does not rank as a first-class dive site. But looking carefully among the patch reefs at 40 feet, you might find small gray morays, blue spotted stingrays, crocodile fish, or a nurse shark. Large groupers and turtles sometimes swim through the area.

SAFAGA AND VICINITY

Safaga is the gateway to the south. Dive boats from Hurghada sometimes come into this area on overnight trips. Primarily a port where freighters unload wheat from the United States, there is one dive center and one hotel. A new tourist village is under construction. Despite its huge port facilities, the town is smaller than Hurghada.

ABU HASHISH is a reef in the mouth of a large bay, with a 40 foot sand plateau broken by small coral heads. Two satellite reefs lie to the outside of the main one. The usual sand creatures can be found among the corals, especially crocodile fish. A sloping dropoff begins at 60 feet. This area is not diveable in heavy wind conditions.

SHARM EL ARAB, a half hour south of Hurghada by car, is one of the few beach dives in the area. Its protected bay also offers an excellent anchorage for overnight boats. Entering from the sandy beach, the bottom drops off immediately into deep water. The sides of the sloping wall are dominated by vertical plate corals. Sand, spilling over the wall from above, inhibits coral growth and reduces visibility below the Red Sea norm. Broken corals along the south wall are a reminder of past incidents of dynamiting. The

best coral formations and reef fish are found from 20 to 60 feet. Along the south wall is a dropoff to 140 feet, but it seems gray and lifeless compared to other areas.

Shallow reefs at the northern end of the bay provide an interesting night dive. Some of the largest basket stars have armspans as big as a diver. Crinoids share the shallow area with the blinking lights of flashlight fish. Sleeping parrotfish and unicorn fish are found in crevices while nocturnal crabs and sea urchins creep along the coral.

A boat is needed to reach the southern point, which is a continuation of the wall. Evidence of recent dynamiting mars the shallow water, with broken corals down to 30 feet. Swarms of parrotfish and striped surgeonfish cruise the wall at that level.

OTA TOBIA, about five miles north of Safaga, is a small sandy island. Sand fleas make it inhospitable for camping. The island is surrounded by four large coral heads rising from sand at 60 feet. A population of garden eels lives in the sandy bottom.

ABU ALAAMA, or PANORAMA REEF, is the best dive site in the Safaga area. A large flat-topped reef just reaching the surface at low tide, its walls drop abruptly into deep water. Enter underneath the marker at the southwest end, then proceed south along the wall at 30 feet to reach an area covered with large anemones. These provide residences for thousands of clownfish, perhaps the greatest concentration in the Red Sea. An area of 20 square meters is filled with anemones and clownfish. Tiny black damselfish share the refuge with the orange twobar anemonefish. Moving back toward the marker, a cave at 20 feet had the thickest concentration of sweepers I have ever seen. From inside, I could actually hear them swimming around my head, sounding like the wings of a swarm of birds or insects.

Below on the sheer wall, a huge black coral tree grows from a crevice at 120 feet. Small mussels grow on its branches, and goldfish flutter around it. The wall continues quite deep, but some of the best scenery is on a plateau at 60 feet, with scattered outcrops decorated by soft corals. An undercut section of the wall continues down to 200 feet.

The northern end of the reef drops off to a sandy plateau at 60 feet. From a large coral head, a gigantic sea fan, over 15 feet across, stands vertically. It is overgrown with small soft corals, and dozens of pastel- colored crinoids perch on it. A swarm of goldfish surrounds the sea fan, while schools of fish form a living ribbon overhead.

South of Panorama Reef, ABU HALHAL is a twin reef rising from a 60-foot sand bottom. This is one of the few which has been attacked by the Crown of Thorns starfish. It has also been dyna-mited, leaving ugly scars. This area is usually dived just to break up a long trip to somewhere else.

DIVING ITINERARY FOR HURGHADA

When based in Hurghada, you can make day trips on charter boats and return to the hotel each night. This restricts diving oppor-tunities to the reefs which can be reached in two hours or less from the port. Night dives would not be possible because boats are not allowed to return to port between sunset and dawn; these require overnight trips. Yet, if amenities are a major concern, this could be a good way to make the first Red Sea trip in ease and comfort. The order of dives is subject to wind and weather conditions.

Day one: El Bareema and Small Giftun Island
Day two: Abu Rimata and Ota Abu Rimata
Day three: Omo Gamaar and Shabroor om Gamaar
Day four: Abu Nuhas (two dives)
Day five: Small Giftun (two dives)
Day six: Carless Reef and Shabroor om Gamaar
Day seven: Repeat any of the above

A more adventurous diver might opt for an itinerary which includes a camping trip to Gubal Island and a crossing to Ras Muhammed.

Day one: Abu Rimata and Ota Abu Rimata
Day two: Omo Gamaar and Shabroor om Gamaar en route to Gubal Island
Day three: Gubal island (three dives, one at night)
Day four: Abu Nuhas (two dives), night dive at Gubal
Day five: Ras Muhammed (three dives, one at night)
Day six: Ras Muhammed (two dives), return to Gubal
Day seven: Shabroor om Gamaar and Carless Reef en route to Hurghada

Additional days can be devoted to day trips out of Hurghada.

*A passenger ship, the Aida, hit the reef at Big Brother
and sank over 50 years ago.*

CHAPTER 7

THE SOUTH

T he south is Egypt's diving frontier. Past Safaga there are no tourist facilities or dive centers, just a two-lane blacktop road heading through barren desert to the Sudan border. Anyone intending to dive this region will need camping gear, food and water, a compressor, and an inflatable boat. The offshore islands require long charter boat trips, often in rough open sea. Heat and hardship will have to be endured, but both biological diversity and reef development increase as you go further south. The result can be rich, unspoiled diving—the way it was before the Red Sea became a tourist destination.

Diving centers don't schedule regular trips to the south; they have to be done by special arrangement. It's a place for people who have been to the Red Sea previously, have seen the best of Sinai and Hurghada, and are looking for new challenges. Two midsea locations, The Brothers and St. John's Island, entail long voyages in uncertain sea conditions. Few divers make the trips. The Brothers trip is presented here in detail to illustrate one of the Red Sea's greatest adventures.

An anchor marks the site of an old shipwreck on Big Brother Island. Our fishing boat is moored beside the pier.

The Brothers: Gems of the Red Sea

On a chart of the Red Sea they are two small dots, about a hundred miles south of Ras Muhammed. Calling them islands is an exaggeration; they are little more than large rocks. Yet, to those who know the area, The Brothers are the stuff of legends. Coral islets atop seamounts arising from out of the abyss, they stand alone in mid sea. Marine life there is said to be the most prolific in the Red Sea, generally considered the world's foremost underwater paradise. The islands can be reached only during infrequent lulls in the prevailing northerly winds that blow out of the Gulf of Suez. Shipwrecks there attest to the fury of sudden storms. The distance, the slow boats, the difficulty of the voyage, and lack of an anchorage limit visitors. These factors have combined to preserve the marine environment's rich, wild and unspoiled state.

In Arabic, they are called Al Ikhwan. The official English names are North and South Island, but when 1984 was right around the corner, we dubbed them Big Brother and Little

174

Brother. Little Brother is a large rock surrounded by a fringing coral reef. A mile away is the larger of the islands, about 400 meters long and nearly rectangular. Once a submerged coral reef, the flat-topped limestone island rises about 30 feet above sea level. A lighthouse dominates the middle. A fringing reef also surrounds Big Brother, the water at the edge dropping off into a deep azure blue. Next to its ramshackle pier, a narrow slot has been blasted in the reef, offering minimal protection for our small boat.

The lighthouse was built by the British in 1883. Its walls of cemented stone are four feet thick at the base, tapering to about two feet at the top. Mohammed Harga, captain of the lighthouse crew, revealed that the government had planned to tear it down several years ago. But inspection proved it to be so structurally sound that nothing comparable could be economically built today. With no electricity on the island, it still operates the same way it did 100 years ago.

Chance Brothers of Birmingham built the light and the mechanism that runs it. A tribute to British workmanship during the Industrial Revolution, the mechanism is a giant clockwork. Its polished walnut and glass case belongs in a museum rather than a working lighthouse in the space age. It is full of brass and stainless steel gears, flywheels and escapements, like a pocket watch on a grand scale. A weight, suspended on a steel cable, is wound with a hand crank to the top of the lighthouse. When a lever is thrown, it begins a leisurely four-hour descent to the bottom, driving the finely balanced fresnel lens mechanism that magnifies the light 200 times. Although weighing over a ton, the four-sided lens can be turned by hand along its circular track. A curtain protects it from the direct rays of the sun during daytime. Despite a few scratches and chips, it looks as though it will still be working after most of us are gone.

The lens amplifies the flame of a gas mantle lantern. Just before sunset, Captain Mohammed led us up the iron spiral staircase to show how it's done. His eyes lit with pride as he pointed out every nuance of the machinery in eloquent but broken English. He rarely has the opportunity to entertain guests

Built by the British in 1884, the lighthouse still operates despite efforts to replace it with an automated one.

Seen from the lighthouse balcony, Big Brother's fringing reef ends in a sheer dropoff.

during the long tour of duty on Big Brother, so everything was meticulously demonstrated. The light itself is like a huge Coleman lantern, powered by white gas that is hand-pumped from a tank below. After a 15- minute warmup period, the full pressure is released and the mantle glows with a white light. The lens begins to turn, focusing the light into four beams which can be seen over a 20-mile radius. It completes a circuit in 20 seconds, so a mariner will see a flash every five seconds.

"A simple job under difficult conditions," is the way Mohammed described his work. His crew of four men are on the island for four-month shifts. With no electricity or fresh water, they are dependent upon a supply ship which arrives every six weeks, Inshallah (God willing). The ship brings them fresh water which is stored in holding tanks that attract every cockroach on the island. Food is bought with each man's meal allowance, amounting to six pounds a week. "We often have to go into our own pockets for food money," he said, but added that they get extra pay for Red Sea duty. When asked why he worked here, the captain replied, "The sea, the solitude, escape from problems." After a tour of duty at the Brothers, he will have two months in Alexandria with his wife and children before being assigned to another lighthouse.

Mohammed stressed the importance of getting along. "If you don't," he smiled, "there is no place to go." In case of emergency, communication is difficult. The only radio was an old Marconi wireless that hasn't worked for years. Once, when a crew member became seriously ill, they made a fire from gasoline and old tires to signal for a boat.

It became obvious that dedication was a major factor in keeping the Brothers light operating. Mohammed and his crew take their work seriously, feeling a kinship with lighthouse keepers everywhere. He inquired about American lighthouses and seemed sad when told that most of them are automated. Eectricity was to come to the Brothers in 1984, in the form of a generator. The old clockwork would be retired, and a more powerful light would replace the gas mantle. Despite the promise of easier work, he seemed wistful about the ending of an era.

Some 20 years ago, President Nasser stopped at the Brothers during a Red Sea cruise. "He took tea with us," said Mohammed with intense pride, "made with our hands, not those of his valets." We also took tea with the Brothers crew. On the last day of our trip, one of the dive guides shot three groupers for lunch. Lacking a boat, the crew normally subsists on small fish they catch from the pier. A grouper is a rare treat, so they pulled out all the stops to set up a farewell banquet. It was one of the finest meals I enjoyed in Egypt. The fish was prepared three different ways: broiled on an open fire with spices, baked with tomatos and onions, and boiled in a spicy sauce. Rice dishes, vegetables and watermelon rounded out the meal, which was served on tablecloths, with everyone dressed in their Friday best. Nasser never had it so good.

But it wasn't the lighthouse that had brought us to the Brothers; it was the underwater environment. Jacques Cousteau stopped there on his first Red Sea expedition, and described the reefs as being populated with "nervous sharks." Because of the distance

The observant diver will glance occasionally toward open water to spot pelagic creatures swimming by, like this sea turtle.

and the difficulty of the crossing, few have tried it since. Stories circulating about the Brothers talked of manta rays, schools of hammerhead sharks, and the mating of large groupers. It is said to be the equal of Ras Muhammed, considered by many to be the best diving spot in the world.

Looking down from the lighthouse balcony at the fringing reef and the sheer drop into crystalline blue water, we knew this was going to be great diving. The first jump off the boat confirmed it. Black coral, beginning at 20 feet, was a sure sign that man hadn't yet made his impact on this environment. Some of the older colonies were overgrown with soft corals, generating impressionistic displays of color. The fish were far bolder than their counterparts at some of the more popular diving locations. A pair of barracuda chased their prey, seemingly oblivious to our presence. A school of tuna, cruising along the wall, bared their teeth at the strange, clumsy intruders. Large schools of surgeon-fish displayed their spines. After hearing about an diver who had been severely cut by one here, we gave them some healthy respect.

Today, the Aida's *deck is a beautiful coral garden.*

The frantic fish activity was most pronounced near sunset as each animal chased the day's final meal, all the while wary of larger predators. Somehow the most efficient predator, man, is ignored because he doesn't fit into the equation here.

The shallow waters around the north end of Big Brother are strewn with wreckage, overgrown after many years underwater. Following the slope of the wall, we come upon the hulls of two ships lying on the steep slope beginning at 90 feet and continuing deeper than any prudent diver would want to go. One is a freighter, about which little is known. The other is a passenger ship, the *Aida*. Judging from the marine growth, she has been down at least 30 years. Soft corals growing from every structure, ventilator horn, and stairway make the wreck an abstract garden of color. In our nitrogen-induced reverie, the deck, covered with small white anemones, reminds us of a ski slope.

A room at the stern has been sheared off by the impact with the reef. The portholes, glass still intact, are open. A large grouper, irritated by the intrusion, swims past us toward open water. Drifting along the deck and down the stairways of the ghost ship, we ponder the tranquility below. It contrasts with the signs of violence at the shallower levels, where wreckage and destruction mar the reef for a quarter-mile area. In the engine room at 140 feet, I film Mia silhouetted in a skylight, surrounded by schooling silver sweepers. Ascending from there, we glance down the deck and spot the outline of the ship's wheel another 50 feet below. Time, depth, and the dive tables prevent a closer look.

Even decompression after a deep dive is enchanting. The sheer wall reaches the surface, and we drift with the current at the 20- and 10-foot levels, watching the colorful scenery go by. The fish activity, ranging from swarms of *Anthias* to frenzied schools of surgeonfish, is the richest and most active I have seen in the Red Sea. Giant sea fans, caves, crevices and overgrown wreck-

FACTS ON THE BROTHERS

Summer weather offers the best chance to make the trip successfully The greatest problem is lack of a protected anchorage for a large boat. On the other hand, wind chop and swells make a ride in a small boat less comfortable.

On Big Brother, which runs on a northwest-southeast axis, the best diving is along the sheer southwestern wall. Its outstanding feature is the tremendous concentration of sea life. Current usually runs southward, so divers are dropped at the northwest end, then drift back to the anchorage. The anchorage is a haven for coronetfish and triggerfish, probably attracted by fish guts thrown off the pier. Look for them at the 10-foot level. Both shipwrecks are at the northern end of the island. The wall on the northeastern side slopes more gradually, and is often swept by stronger currents. Don't waste your time there on a short trip.

Little Brother has sheer walls with caves, big sea fans and lots of fish activity. If you stay shallow, 40 feet or less, you can swim around the entire island on one dive. Watch which way the current is running and plan the dive accordingly, especially if decompression is necessary.

age seem to go by as the current returns us to the pier.

We never saw any nervous sharks, only an occasional individual cruising in the distance. It was also the wrong time of year for manta rays, so that facet of the Brothers' undersea life will have to wait for another trip. That will mean sleeping on the ramshackle pier, covered with dew from nightfall until the northerly winds begin to blow around two AM. It means bringing all our own food and water because the lighthouse crew's meager rations can't be shared. After a week of saltwater baths, we will long for the comforts of civilization and wonder how the crew can take four months of isolation here. But with the passage of time, discomfort is forgotten.

The images remaining are joyful ones: the spectacular undersea life and the warm hospitality of the lighthouse crew. One image persists. Lying on the pier in my sleeping bag, I look up at the stars of the Milky Way, pierced by the four revolving beams of the lighthouse. I think about how lucky we have been to be here, at this time, and wonder what will happen when larger, faster boats bring more and more casual visitors.

THE SOUTH

The drive south can be broken up with beach dives along the way. Look for coves from the road, especially along the routes of old dry washes. The best beach diving is usually off the points, with the southern point generally better than the northern one.

Qeseir is the southernmost major town on the Egyptian Red Sea coast. It has a good harbor with lots of small fishing boats, but no tourist facilities. Food and basic supplies can be bought there. Trips to The Brothers can originate from Qeseir on a boat brought down from Hurghada or Safaga. An ancient Roman port, OLD QESEIR HARBOR, is located north of town; it is said that amphoras and other artifacts can still be found there. If so, they are buried under two thousand years' accumulation of sediment. The sloping wall drops abruptly to over 130 feet, but the best diving is shallow, with many macro subjects. Look in the shallow crevices for pipefish, scorpionfish, lizardfish and big serpulids (Christmas tree worms).

From inside a cave on Little Brother, the visibility exceeds 200 feet.

About an hour beyond Qeseir by car is a small mining town, MARSA ALAM. On the beach is the guest house of a shooting club, equipped with facilities to sleep a dozen people. A resident cook and two servants are there to take care of visitors who have made prior reservations with the club. They can supply a fishing boat or an inflatable to take divers to nearby reefs. Since this is the only diving spot in the south with creature comforts, Egyptian divers come down here fairly often.

Unfortunately, it is not patrolled. A few scions of wealthy families take advantage of the fact and spear reef fish on scuba. Bringing brand new tanks and compressors, along with heavy artillery straight out of the box, these "sportsmen" test their limited experience and skill on the big, docile groupers which have seldom seen divers. Few of the dead fish are eaten; most are given away. The results are apparent when diving on the main reef some 1-1/2 miles off the beach, SHA'AB ALAM. There are no big fish left, and the small ones are generally spooky. More education and enforcement are needed to stop these practices, which could spoil an underwater paradise. Sha'ab Alam is about 300 yards long, with the top exposed at low tide. The sloping

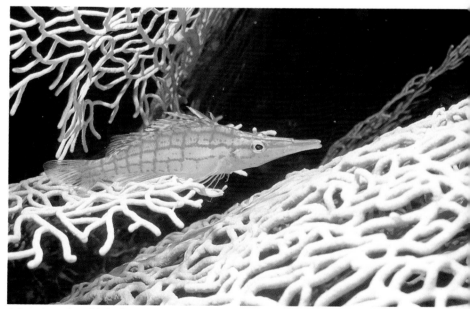

A longnose hawkfish, Oxycirrhites typus, *hides within a sea fan. These fishes are generally found in deeper water.*

wall drops to 60 feet in sand. Surgeonfish, snappers and yellow grunts school around the reef. It bears old scars of dynamite fishing. Satellite reef pinnacles surround the main one, with far better invertebrate growth and fish life.

Some 300 yards from the main reef, OTA ALAM seems to have escaped the attention of the hunters. It has some of the richest growth of soft corals I have seen in the Red Sea. Smaller than Sha'ab Alam, it rises from sand at 70 feet, with the top 10 feet below the surface. Several satellite reefs surround it, coral pillars with 35 feet of vertical relief. They look like enchanted towers out of *Lord of the Rings*. Lush soft corals in yellows and purples cover broad areas, including one entire wall. Caves, table corals, and other hard corals are everywhere. One cave has a high arching entrance, like the one at Ras Atar in Sinai. It's a great frame for diver pictures. Schools of masked surgeonfish, snappers, and jacks surround the reef. Sharks are commonly seen swimming in the distance. A huge tuna, attracted by the activity, circled me here for several minutes. On another dive, I joined a school of large barracuda for a short decompression stop.

WADI EL LUEILI offers beach camping and several reefs a mile offshore, that can be dived from an inflatable. On the seaward side of the reefs, the walls drop to a shelf from 80 to 100 feet, then slope deeper. Marine life in the south generally is richer, with the fish calmer and not used to divers. More sharks and barracuda are seen as you go further south. Wadi El Lueili is a typical example. Its best features are the beauty of the cove, the abundance of schooling fish, and the concentration of hard and soft corals.

Forty miles south of Marsa Alam is WADI EL GEMAL, a small seaside oasis surrounding a lake of brackish water. Old tombs of sheikhs overlook the lake. Don't camp there, because poisonous snakes and mosquitoes inhabit the area. A small government fishing project is located nearby. The natives are very reserved and prefer to be left alone.

A large island, lying a couple of miles offshore, can be reached easily in an inflatable. Watch out for shallow reefs along

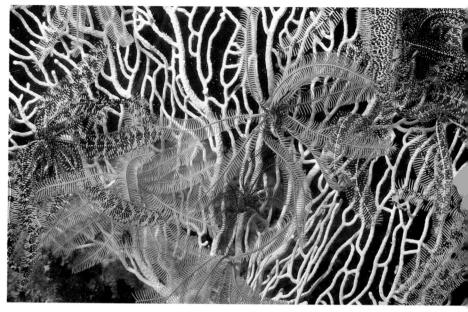

A large sea fan is covered with pastel-colored crinoids.

the way. You can camp on the island, which is protected by a fringing reef. There are several small "swimming pools" on the reef shelf. Some of them go all the way through to deep water. Big groupers or sharks may sometimes encountered in the pools or in the passageways. That makes for exciting diving, even in bad weather. When conditions are calm, dive along the reef wall for glimpses of sharks. The wall drops to 60 feet on the seaward side, and is frequented by schools of jacks, solitary groupers, and other big fish. At night, lots of lobsters can be seen in the shallows.

The ruins of an old lighthouse are on the point at RAS HONKORAB. It makes a good campsite, right next to the diving area. The fringing reef to the south of the point has a shallow pool with a sandy bottom, nine to 12 feet deep. Its protected water is excellent for snorkelers. The wide reef ends in a wall dropping to 60 feet, then sloping off into deep water. Coral patches in the sand offer a calm, protected area for beginning and intermediate level divers. You are very likely to see reef sharks swimming by in this area.

185

DIVING EMERGENCIES

We hope you will never have to use the procedures outlined here. But the Egyptian Red Sea is a frontier area, and the emergency response system is still primitive in some places. This puts more responsibility on the individual to dive conservatively and follow safe practices. Remember, diving accidents are far easier to prevent than to treat.

Two double-lock recompression chambers were available for sport divers in the Egyptian Red Sea at the time this was written. One is in Eilat, Israel, and the other at Magaweesh Tourist Village near Hurghada. The former serves the Sinai; the other the Hurghada area and the south. Chambers are also located on some of the oil platforms in the Gulf of Suez, but at present they are available only to oil company personnel.

Despite political tensions, the Israeli chamber stands ready to help in case of problems. A trained crew is on call, and border formalities are waived in emergencies. Helicopter transportation is provided by the MFO (Multinational Force and Observers). They can be contacted by the dive centers through VHF radio, by telephone, or in person at their base south of Naama Bay. Response time from pickup to the chamber is about an hour.

The Magaweesh facility is available to any victim of a diving accident regardless of origin. There are plans to establish a chamber at one of the dive centers in Sinai, and also one in Hurghada. But at the present time they are still in the talking stage.

While waiting for transportation to a chamber, the victim should be laid on an incline, with the feet about eighteen inches higher than the head. Most dive guides carry oxygen, which should be administered to the victim if available.

Throughout this volume, the reader has been cautioned to watch depth and bottom times. There are marvelous sights at depth in the Red Sea. But the emergency response network is not as reliable as that in more developed locations. Intelligent diving practices will prevent your having to depend on it. The responsibility for safety rests with you.

The masked puffer, Arothron diadematus, *sleeps on a coral head.*

ST. JOHN'S ISLAND (ZABARGHAD ISLAND) lies in mid sea near the Sudanese border. It is a 12-hour trip from Abu Ghoussoun in a small boat, in uncertain sea conditions. The journey is part of the adventure. Dr. Adel Taher spent 28 days there in 1975. He reports, "The boatman who took us swore on his mother's grave he would never go there again." The boat was filled with water containers; for food they planned to subsist on fish. Three attempts to return to the mainland were aborted due to rough sea conditions. On the fourth they had to go for it, because the fresh water was gone.

The island's history dates back to the Ptolemaic pharaohs. Peridot, a green semiprecious stone, was mined there. In order to keep the location secret, passing ships were captured and the crews enslaved to work in the mine. Some attempts were made to reopen the mine in the early 20th century, but were stopped after the 1952 revolution. Adel and his friends climbed the island's high peak to collect splinters of peridot left over from the operation.

The best time to make the trip is during August and September. A barrier reef protects the sandy beach on the east side of the island. Sea turtles lay their eggs there in large numbers; there is also a seagull rookery. Tunnels and caves cut through the barrier reef into the shallow lagoon. On the outside, a sloping wall drops to 115 feet. Black corals grow all along it, even in shallow water. Reef sharks cruise along the wall along with schools of jacks, surgeonfish, and occasional big gamefish. The southern end of the island has a sheer, deep wall, but calm weather is needed to dive it. Adel admits, however, that although a trip to St. John's is high adventure, diving is better at The Brothers.

South of Ras Benas is an area of scattered reefs called Foul Bay. Its many reefs constitute a navigation hazard. One of them, WHITE ROCK, is topped off by an irregular rock that looks like a boat. It is surrounded by a fringing reef, dropping to a plateau at 50 feet with beautiful coral pillars rising almost to the surface. The plateau ends in a wall dropping to 150 feet. Fish and invertebrate life is rich and colorful. Dr. Taher describes the fish as being so bold that, "..you get the feeling you are the first to have dived there." If not the first, you would certainly be one of the few, in an area well off the beaten path.

ITINERARY FOR THE SOUTH

A trip by car would run about six days, with two-day stops in each area. If more time is available the trip could continue further south, perhaps hiring a boat at Port Berenice for a trip to White Rock. The six day itinerary:

Days one and two: Marsa Alam
Days three and four: Wadi El Gemal
Days five and six: Head back north, stopping at Wadi El Lueili

A longer journey can combine this itinerary with a boat trip to St. John's Island or to White Rock.

A boat trip to the Brothers can leave from Hurghada, Safaga or Qeseir. Allow at least three days to dive the islands, plus two traveling days. A six- or seven-day trip would be ideal. St.

John's can be reached from Ras Benas or Port Berenice, allowing about the same time frame. Since both journeys involve long crossings in open sea, and are extremely dependent on favorable weather, they should be made during the summer months.

Notes on Photographs

Following slide presentations on this material, I have often been asked about the equipment used. Choices of cameras and films are extremely subjective, but for what it's worth, here is the technical information on the photos in this book. They were shot over a six year period, from 1982 through 1988. During that time, the camera system has evolved, as well as techniques. In the end, I was using the equipment described below.

Topside photography was done with a Nikon Ftn and an FE, utilizing Nikkor 20, 24, 50, and 55-macro lenses, as well as a Vivitar 70-210 mm zoom. Two were shot with an Olympus Infinity automated 35 mm camera. Films utilized included Kodachrome 64, Ektachrome 64 Professional, Fujichrome 50 and 100 Professional and Ektachrome 400.

Underwater, two systems were used. Marine life closeups were shot with a Nikon F and 55mm Micro-Nikkor lens, encased in a Giddings Nikko-Mar housing. The housing was modified by Gates Underwater Products, San Diego, who installed a hemispherical dome port. Strobes used included Ikelite Substrobe 150, Oceanic 2003, and SR 2000. All closeups were taken with two strobes.

Wide-angle pictures were shot with a Nikonos III, 15mm and 28 mm lenses. Ambient light metering was done with a Sekonic 164B. The Nikon 28mm lens was utilized for extension tube photography. Film used during the last two years was Fujichrome 50 and 100 Professional.

DIVE GEAR CHECKLIST

Dive centers in Egypt can supply you with tanks, weights, and usually with backpacks. Most also have regulators, buoyancy compensators and wetsuits available for rent. However, it is best to bring along equipment that you are familiar with, even if you have to pay excess baggage charges for a backpack and BC combination. Included here is an equipment checklist for divers traveling to the Red Sea.

DIVING EQUIPMENT

Gear bags: A heavy-duty bag for the airplane, a mesh bag for boats

Wetsuit: Eighth-inch (3mm) for summer, quarter-inch (7mm) for winter

Regulator, including console and octopus (In case of second stage problems, the octopus can substitute or be used for parts if compatible)

Console gauges: Pressure gauge, depth gauge, compass, timer, computer

Buoyancy compensator, including spare inflator hose

Backpack (with bands capable of holding 90-cubic-foot tanks)

Mask, fins, snorkel

Boots (sturdy enough for walking over coral)

Gloves

Watch

Slate and pencil

Dive tables, printed on plastic

Underwater light and spare batteries

SPARE PARTS KIT

Everything in this kit will fit into a small plastic box.
Silicone grease
Assorted O rings
Silicone spray
WD-40
Screwdriver, pliers, crescent wrench
Tie wraps
Mask and fin straps
Swiss Army knife
Waterproof marking pen
Plastic bags

FIRST AID KIT:

Everything in this and the spare parts kit will fit in a small tackle box.

Adhesive bandages
Triangular bandage
Adhesive tape
Sterile dressings
Steri-strips
Aspirin
Decongenstant
Seasickness medication

Antibiotic ointment
Diarrhea medication
Sunscreen
Lip balm with sunscreen
Germicidal liquid soap
Alcohol
Elastic bandage
Any necessary prescriptions

A tiny spider crab walks along a soft coral, apparently immune to its sting.

Most Red Sea crabs are nocturnal. This one is Carpilius convexus.

Chapter 8

Night Diving

S unset. You are comfortable, warm and dry, sipping tea on the carpeted floor of the dining tent while the wind from out of the Gulf of Suez howls outside. You have had a good day of diving the wrecks of Abu Nuhas, baked awhile in the desert sun, swapped tall tales with your buddies and the Egyptian guides. The equipment has been put away and all you want to do now is relax until dinner. You know that dinner is a major affair, and it will be served late, according to local custom. The last thing in the world you want to do right now is to climb back into that wet, smelly suit and go night diving.

Sound familiar? We all fall prey to that warm, comfortable feeling on occasion. But in the Red Sea, that feeling can cheat you out of some of the best diving the area has to offer. In many places around the globe, nightlife is not much different from that found by day. But the Red Sea becomes another world after dark. As the light beam focuses your attention, your senses are more sharply tuned to every stimulus. Your entire consciousness is centered around the cone of your flashlight beam.

It isn't quite as easy here as it would be at home or in a well-developed resort area. Egypt is extremely security conscious, as

When it comes to instant color changes, the cuttlefish outperforms even its cousin, the octopus.

are most Middle Eastern nations. Exit and entry is limited from a harbor or a beach after dark, and many of the popular places are patrolled. The concern is more with smugglers and drug runners than with spies. But nevertheless, it doesn't pay to argue with people carrying guns, especially when it's their country. So the best way to go night diving is to stay overnight on a boat, or to camp on one of the desert islands.

Camping with an Egyptian dive operation isn't exactly the way it was in Boy Scouts, though. First, they do all the work, including KP. The tents are a big improvement over GI issue; tall canvas wall tents with colorful roofs and fringes. With the carpeted floors and electric lights, you feel like Lawrence of Arabia. Our camp was located on Gubal Island, at the mouth of the Gulf of Suez.

I traveled with the advance party to set up camp. Our small Egyptian fishing boat looked like a seagoing version of a Model T from the dustbowl days. Mattresses, boxes of provisions, carpets and compressors were piled and lashed to every square foot of deck space. There was barely room to move around. Led by Captain Moued, a thin, wiry fisherman with a limited vocabulary of broken English, the crew looked like a bunch of pirates. What they lacked in language, however, they made up in seamanship. Consulting neither map nor compass, Moued unerringly guided the 30-foot vessel around reefs and through passages in the moonless night. The sea was flat and calm. I lay on the mattress looking up at the Milky Way, amazed at the vast numbers of stars which filled the desert sky.

As we approached the fringing reef around Gubal Island, the two-banger diesel slowed to trolling speed, but the activity level of the crew picked up. With no lights to illuminate the winding passage through the reef, a lookout on the bow called instructions back to the tillerman, all the while watching for the dark patches which indicated deeper water. "Mashi!" was the word that meant "OK." A tension-filled twenty minutes of zigzags and course changes were punctuated only with the directions from the lookout. My respect for Egyptian seamanship grew with each "Mashi." Finally, the keel dug into beach sand, and we had arrived on Gubal Island.

Gubal is the jumping off place for some of the finest diving in the Red Sea. The dropoffs of Carless Reef, the tame groupers and Napoleon Wrasses of Shabroom Om Gamaar, and the wrecks of Abu Nuhas are just an hour or so away. The island itself has a fringing coral reef and a shallow wreck on the lee side. The windward side is a dropoff, with the wreck of a large freighter lying on the slope. Groupers and Napoleons frequent the deep wreck, about 90 feet down. Both areas are excellent night diving spots, and that's another reason to camp on Gubal.

Driven by the tales of the guides and the other divers, you reluctantly leave the tent, climb into the cold, damp suit, and join the others on the boat. The passage through the reef now marked with buoys, the skipper chugs his diesel toward the island's northern point. The anchor drops, and everyone is ready. No matter how often you have done it, there is always a touch of apprehension before jumping into the dark water. You check your gear with just a little more care and, once underwater, stay just a bit closer to your buddy. But as you descend and your light beam

The shallow waters are the realm of the basket stars, Astroboa nuda.

Asthenosoma varium *is a colorful, but poisonous sea urchin. A sting from its spines causes burning pain.*

paints the reefs with color, subliminal fears are forgotten. The brilliant colors of the Red Sea are even more striking when illuminated directly, without the filtering effect of many feet of water overhead. You are in an underwater fantasyland, wondering how different the familiar reef will look now that the night creatures have taken over.

The shallows are the realm of the basket stars. Nearly everywhere we point our lights, the beam illuminates their gnarled tentacles, sifting the water column for plankton. They are some of the largest I have ever seen, with armspans almost as long as my body. During the day, these nocturnal echinoderms are seldom noticed, remaining curled in an inconspicuous ball. But at night they dominate the upper reaches of the reef, looking like Medusa's head of snakes. When hit by my light beam, the reaching arms begin to curl and retract, as if being burned by the light. Although I realize the creatures are quite harmless, the

196

reaction reminds me of the vampire legends when Dracula recoiled from the light of the sun.

Basket stars share their territory with another strange echinoderm, the crinoid. Although crinoids are found in all oceans of the world, many are out of diving range. The Red Sea's varieties are common in shallow water, both night and day. Colors range from deep primary shades to delicate pastels and multicolored patterns. During the day many are coiled, others rest passively on gorgonians or soft corals, feathery arms spread out flat. But at night they perch on the shallow reefs, arms slowly waving in the current to catch planktonic creatures. Occasionally dissatisfied with its hunting, a crinoid will fly to another coral head by delicately undulating its 10 to 40 arms. How such a primitive creature can coordinate so many appendages is one of the sea's great mysteries. Crinoids are true living fossils, having changed little since the Cambrian Age, some 600 million years ago.

From the surface, we could see many lights blinking and flashing below. They weren't the tiny sparklers one usually sees in nighttime waters, but large, bright, cold blue lights. Underwater, the same lights can be seen around the reef, especially when we turn off our own. Called "Le Petit Puegeot" by the French because they look like miniature automobile headlights, they belong to *Photoblepharon*, the flashlight fish. Only three inches long, the tiny fishes usually swim about the reef in pairs. A pouch below each eye contains millions of luminescent bacteria, similar to those that cause the glow of fireflies. As a matter of fact, flashlight fish look like giant fireflies when seen in total darkness. By momentarily covering the pouch with a flap of skin, they can blink their lights. This action confounds and confuses predators, because the nervous little fish dart about while flashing. The predator, whether a large fish or a larger diver, is easily frustrated chasing such elusive prey.

On a normal dive, one can expect to see perhaps a dozen flashlight fish, one or two pairs at a time. When spotting our first ones, we were really excited, because we hadn't considered it a real Red Sea night dive without them. But one moonless night at the Brothers Islands, the water surrounding the reefs was alive

A pouch below the flashlight fish's eye contains luminescent bacteria, which emit a powerful glow at night. Note its large eyes, typical of creatures living at low light levels.

with lights. It was an underwater fireworks display, as hundreds of tiny crescents pierced the darkness, bathing the reef in an eerie blue light. Obviously, the ambient light level has a lot of effect on the activity of *Photoblepharon*. When it's really dark, they seem to be everywhere.

The reclusive creatures swim for cover when a light beam is pointed their way. In order to approach them closely, turn off your lamp. Then follow the fish into a shallow crevice to corner them, and turn on the light to see their bodies. Photographing *Photoblepharon*, must also be done in total darkness. Prefocus the camera for a foot or two, then aim for the crescents in the viewfinder. It's a hit and miss affair, with lots more misses than hits.

Flashlight fishes have been observed in the Caribbean, ascending to the 200-foot level at night. But in the Red Sea, they come up into shallow waters. Your first sighting of flashlight fish is one you will long remember. They alone make it worthwhile to go diving at night.

The world's largest nudibranch, Hexabranchus sanguinea, *grows to over a foot in length.*

Rarely seen during the daylight hours, crabs of many varieties roam the reefs at night looking for food. Tiny white spider crabs march across the soft corals, looking like snow-covered Daddy Long Legs. Orange-hued crabs, about the size of a fist, remind one of cartoon characters as they stare back at the diver, claws ready for defense. But perhaps the most unusual specimen is the decorator crab. For camouflage, he attaches tiny gorgonians, soft corals, and other marine life to his carapace. Thus attired, he waits for unwary prey to blunder along. Only as he moves away from the diver's light does his presence become obvious.

Imagine a nudibranch about a foot long that swims through the water column by undulating its body. No, that's not a nitrogen induced fantasy, but the Spanish Dancer. Colored a deep shade of red with a white fringe, this nocturnal mollusc is sometimes seen feeding on soft corals. When disturbed, it swims away. The undulating waves passing through its body cause the white trim on its scarlet mantle to look like the skirts of a Flamenco dancer.

As the nighttime fishes roam the reefs, the day shift sleeps in crevices within the coral. Large parrotfish, skittish by day, can be photographed in wide-eyed slumber. Protected from predators and parasites by a mucus cocoon, their fused front teeth are displayed in a mocking grin. Often they can be touched and petted while sleeping, but sometimes will awake suddenly and bolt. When that happens, it's a tossup as to who has had the greatest shock, the fish or the diver.

Almost blending into the reef, the venomous scorpionfish lies quietly in the open, waiting to ambush an unwary crab. Down in the sand, the shy unicornfish sleeps soundly and can be approached much closer than is possible by day. Large spotted groupers prefer caves. If disturbed by a light or a strobe, they just bare their teeth and look angry, but do nothing to back it up.

The dangers of night diving in the Red Sea are often unexpected ones. One evening our boat set off to dive the shallow wreck at Gubal Island. Having previously dove it at night, my buddy, Mike Curtis, and I talked our dive guide into dropping us off at the north wall while his customers dove the shallows. He sent a crew member, Hani, to accompany us in a Zodiac. We thought this was totally unnecessary and not in keeping with our image as macho divers. Before descending, we told Hani we didn't need him, and suggested he take the Zodiac back to the dive boat.

Descending to 80 feet on the wall, we noticed a bit of a current. As the textbooks advise, we decided to begin the dive upcurrent, then ride it back to our entry point. But Red Sea currents sometimes ignore the textbooks. At first, this one was just mildly irritating as we gave our attention to sleeping parrotfish and drowsy groupers. We followed some *Photoblepharon*, into a small cave, trying to read our instruments by the blue light of their photophores. Turning on our flashlights, we saw for the first time that they are small brown fish, with iridescent blue markings around their heads. A large sea slug in a hole looked like a Spanish Dancer, but upon pulling it out we discovered a case of mistaken identity. By this time, the current had become stronger and had progressed from the irritant to the hassle stage. Our air over half gone, we ascended to 40 feet and

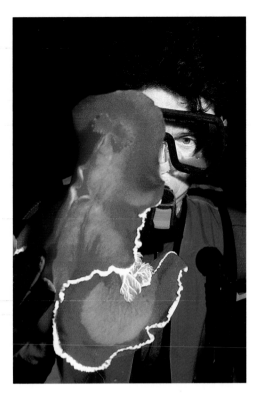

The Spanish Dancer's undulating swimming movements and the white fringe around its body suggest a flamenco dancer.

decided to go with the current for a while, holding on when we saw something interesting. After a few minutes of this, things were getting unpleasant enough for us to abandon our ideas and surface. We had overshot the starting point and were drifting in the general direction of Hurghada. The lights of the boat seemed a long way off and, despite a lot of grunting and kicking, weren't getting any closer. We might be swimming yet, except that Hani hadn't listened to us and was still out there with the Zodiac. A couple of thoroughly chastened macho divers, we eagerly accepted his offer of a lift.

You often appreciate things more if they don't come easily. Returning to camp from the night dive, the wind is still blowing out of the Gulf of Suez. You are cold and wet, and will still be salty in the morning. But you relish the memories of the color, the variety and the excitement of the Red Sea after dark. Tomorrow night you may again be reluctant to leave the warmth and comfort of your tent. But you will. And you feel sorry for your friends in their warm beds who missed this experience.

You haven't really seen the pyramids until you view them from the back of a camel.

202

Chapter 9

Footloose in Egypt

T oday's traveler to Egypt is following a long procession of tourists stretching back across the ages. The pyramids were already over 2,000 years old when Alexander the Great arrived with his army. But Egyptian tourism didn't begin with Alexander; it had already been going on for centuries. Many of the ancient monuments are marked with graffiti from Greeks, Romans, early Christians, and Europeans.

When you go to the Red Sea to dive, don't miss Egypt. Set aside a few days — or a couple of weeks if possible — to go back through the corridors of time and see the beginnings of civilization. The entire country is a living museum. Not only are there the stone remnants of the pharaohs, but life along the Nile continues much the same as it did hundreds of years ago.

The Greek historian Herodotus, writing in the fifth century BC, called Egypt "the gift of the Nile." The annual spring floods brought rich black alluvial silt which fertilized the fields along the river. Irrigation canals brought the life-giving water further inland, transforming a fringe of the desert into rich farmland. The ancient name for Egypt was Kemi, or "The Black Land."

Fellucas, the Nile sailing craft, travel south with the prevailing winds. To go north, they drop their sails and drift with the current.

Away from the river and the canals, the desert abruptly reclaims its territory. In some places the greenbelt extends a few kilometers or more beyond the river; in others only a few meters. Not a blade of grass grows in the villages at the edge of the fields, because water is too precious to waste on decoration. Over 95 percent of Egypt's land is uninhabited desert. It's not a pretty desert with cactus and flowers, but a hot, barren wasteland of featureless sand. The remaining five percent of the land houses 95 percent of the country's population of over 50 million. That gives Egypt one of the highest population densities in the world, nearly 5,000 persons per square mile. On a map, the fertile area looks like a lotus plant. The Nile is the stem, the Fayuum Oasis the bud, and the Delta the flower. Red Sea communities lie outside the lotus and exist only because of wells and pipelines from the river, and recently, desalinization plants.

Today the river no longer floods its banks. The Aswan High Dam, built with the help of the Russians and completed in 1971, holds back the waters of 300-mile-long Lake Nasser. Enough electricity is generated to supply most of Egypt's needs, and the

204

flow of water is carefully controlled. It saved Egypt from the drought and famine that afflicted Ethiopia. But the dam has not been an unmixed blessing. Silt no longer flows from the Ethiopian highlands, so synthetic fertilizers are needed to make the crops grow. Fisheries along Egypt's Mediterranean coast have declined because of the lack of nutrients reaching the sea. And ancient monuments are showing damage from higher humidity and salts in the water table.

The population trend today is for people to move away from the rural areas and into the cities. Cairo's population has exploded, and is presently estimated between 14 and 15 million. It is the largest city in Africa, the crossroads of the Middle East, and the cultural and political center of the Arab world. A bustling, vibrant city, Cairo has modern office towers and ancient monuments, palatial mansions and depressing slums.

Your tour of Egypt will most likely begin and end in Cairo. In this chapter we will begin there and take you up the Nile. The journey will take us not only across the miles, but also across the centuries.

CAIRO

When in Cairo, every tourist should see the Sphinx, the Pyramids, and the Egyptian Museum. Given another day, there is the Khan el Khalili Bazaar, The Citadel, and the major mosques, perhaps the Sultan Hassan and Ibn Tulun. Evenings can be devoted to sailing down the Nile on a felucca, dinner in an exotic restaurant, or a sampling of the city's night life. Cairo is incredibly rich with historic buildings and museums which can keep a history buff busy for many days. But for the diver who has an extra week at the end of a Red Sea trip, two to three days in the capitol city is enough. Some time should be saved for Upper Egypt.

Cairo traffic can be heavy at times so allow yourself plenty of time. A car with an English-speaking driver can be arranged for the day through any of the small travel agencies in the city. Check on it at your hotel. If you have confidence in your ability to find your own way, just take a cab. There will be no problem

Painted over 3,000 years ago, the colors on tomb walls are as vivid as if they had been done yesterday.

getting another one for the return trip from any tourist destination.

The MUSEUM OF EGYPTIAN ANTIQUITIES closes at four o'clock, earlier on Fridays or during Ramadan, so it should be the first stop of the day. Built at the turn of the century, the building is poorly ventilated and can become uncomfortable during summer afternoons.

The collection staggers comprehension. Someone figured if you allowed one minute for each exhibit, you could see everything in the Museum in about nine months. It's like an old attic full of priceless historic treasures, including some of the world's greatest art. However, all but the most avid Egyptologist will suffer sensory overload after about three hours. If you are planning on only one visit to the museum, it will have to be a superficial tour of the highlights. The best way to see it, time permitting, is on several trips spread out over a few days. I was fortunate enough to do it this way over five summers, but after about a dozen visits still feel that I have only scratched the surface.

When you buy your ticket outside, be sure to purchase an official guidebook. It describes all the important exhibits, coded to the numbers on the cases. It doesn't describe every exhibit. There are over 100,000 of them, and that would require a lot more than the book's 300 pages. You will be pestered outside by hawkers selling "genuine" antiquities and inside by "official" guides offering their services in English, French, German, or even Japanese. It may be better to do it yourself, at your own pace, referring to the guidebook. If you want more information, just wait awhile until a group shows up with a guide. It costs nothing to listen to the commentary. Since each

The Museum of Egyptian Antiquities is a must for any tourist in Cairo. A serious archaeology student can spend months inside without seeing it all.

guide embellishes a story differently, it can be interesting to hang around an exhibit for more than one version.

Cameras are now allowed inside the museum at an additional charge. However, the museum is too crowded and the lighting too poor to take good photographs. If you really want museum pictures for your Egypt slide show, buy them at the museum gift shop or at the bazaar. They were taken by professionals under optimum conditions and are better than anything we could do under the circumstances. An official catalogue was published in 1987, with text and beautiful color photographs of 270 of the most significant exhibits.

The exhibits are arranged chronologically, beginning on the first floor. Many visitors proceed directly to the second floor, where the Tutankhamen galleries are located. The historic exhibition which traveled around America a few years ago contained about 50 items from the young pharaoh's tomb. All are back in the Museum now, along with about 1,700 more. Most of the important pieces made the trip, but two never left Egypt: the golden throne with an exquisite relief carving of Tutankhamen and his bride; and his innermost coffin, over 400 pounds of solid gold and precious stones. The intricate decoration is displayed in a mirrored case so you can also see the underside. In a case near the coffin is one of the immortal works of art conceived during man's tenure on this planet: the golden mask that covered the head of Tutankhamen's mummy. Across the void of 30 centuries, you can look into the young king's eyes as though he were about to speak to you.

Some of the most touching exhibits are not the golden ones. There are wreaths of brown flowers, seeds, hunting bows, sandals, and even the pharaoh's underwear, which lend a human scale to the grandeur of the treasures.

There is much more to see than Tutankhamen. The main hall contains huge works on a colossal scale. On the ground floor, the Old Kingdom exhibits include the Palette of Narmer, honoring the king who united Upper and Lower Egypt, and a black diorite statue of Chephren, who built the second of the Great Pyramids. Some of the loveliest statues date back to the period of the Old Kingdom. Many pieces will seem familiar as you recognize them from photographs you have seen over the years.

An entire room is dedicated to Akhenaton, the heretic pharaoh who introduced the worship of a single god to Egypt. The artistic style during his reign was more natural and lifelike, contrasting with the idealized way most pharaohs were depicted. Akhenaton's ugliness accentuates the beauty of his queen, Nefertiti, whose statue appears next to his.

Mummies of the pharaohs used to be on display in a room on the first floor. This exhibit was closed several years ago, when they began to show signs of deterioration. An international research project resulted in the development of new display cases that will better preserve the bodies, so they are scheduled to go back on exhibit soon. Numerous mummies of sacred animals, including a huge Nile fish and a 20-foot crocodile, are still on display.

Dating back 4,000 years, the solar boat was buried next to Cheops' pyramid to transport the pharaoh to the afterlife.

On the second floor are some wrapped mummies from the Roman era. Beautiful lifelike portraits, painted on wood, are bound over the mummies' heads. One of the most moving exhibits in the Museum, these ordinary people, black and white, of all ages, seem almost recognizable, like someone you may have met in the street only yesterday.

Entire rooms are devoted just to scarabs, or toiletries, or to papyrus pages from The Book of the Dead. If you hadn't read up on ancient Egypt before coming here, you will wish you had. The problem is that the Museum is just too small and crowded to allow full appreciation of what's inside. It's like a poorly edited slide show. However, a new museum is under construction on Gezirah Island, which will house some of the exhibits. With the collection divided, visitors should be able to gain a better understanding of the scope of Egyptian history.

The GREAT PYRAMIDS OF GIZEH are located on the outskirts of town. Actually, Cairo has expanded to meet its famous monuments. We usually see the pyramids photographed with desert as background but, viewed from the opposite angle, the buildings of suburban Cairo are directly beneath the Gizeh Plateau. Of the Seven Wonders of the Ancient World, only the pyramids still stand. Built 45 centuries ago, they served as the funerary monuments of the Pharaohs Cheops, Chephren and Mycerinus.

A visitor's first reaction to the pyramids can range from mild disappointment to total awe. But after being there awhile and letting the massiveness and the antiquity of the monuments sink in, you realize why people have been attracted to this spot for over 4,000 years. In this span of time, we are closer to Julius Caesar than he was to the builders of the pyramids.

You won't be there long before being besieged by persons selling things, from postcards to camel rides. Take them up on it if you want, but don't forget to bargain. That's part of the game. If you aren't interested, "La, shukran," means "No, thank you".

For a small admission charge, you can go inside Cheops' pyramid. It's not a place for the claustrophobic or the poorly conditioned. There is a small corridor through which you have to squat and duck-walk before reaching the Great Gallery, a true

The Sphinx and Pyramids have seen over 1,600,000 sunsets.

architectural marvel. Your thighs will feel the effects for the next day or so. At the top of the ascending gallery is a chamber where the king's empty sarcophagus stands.

In 1954 an Egyptian archaeologist discovered a 140-foot funerary boat in a trench next to Cheops' pyramid. After nearly 30 years of restoration, the SOLAR BOAT was placed on display in its own concrete and glass building next to the pyramid. Because of the cost of restoration and construction of the air-conditioned building (a modern eyesore next to the ancient monument), there is an admission charge to enter the structure and see the boat. It's worth it. This magnificent vessel is the oldest ship ever found. Its 1,200 pieces were rebuilt using the original methods. No one is sure whether the boat actually carried the Pharaoh's body up the Nile, or whether it was intended for his use in the afterlife. It is beautifully displayed, and cameras are allowed for a slight additional fee.

The SPHINX, at the foot of the Pyramids, recently underwent restoration work because of water damage. Its face is thought to be that of Chephren, the body that of a lion. Contrary to popular legend, it wasn't Napoleon's soldiers who shot the

Natives as well as tourists do their shopping in the crowded streets of the Khan el Khalili Bazaar.

nose off; the Corsican was a staunch admirer of Egyptian history. There is a wall around the sphinx, but if you go inside the Valley Temple, you can get within closeup range. The sphinx faces the rising sun, so morning is the best time for pictures. But you may prefer to come in the afternoon, watch the sunset, and stay for the Sound and Light Show after dark. The monuments close at four o'clock, but you can still do everything except go inside the pyramid and see the Solar Boat.

Late afternoon at the pyramids is a happening. Most of the tourists are gone, so the local people congregate on the shady side and enjoy the evening breeze, smoking their hubble bubbles (water pipes), and discussing the events of the day. Unlike city people, most of them wear galibiyas as they walk their camels, gallop their horses, or picnic in family groups. It's a good natured, relaxed time of day and, wandering among them, you really get the feeling of being in an exotic land.

The SOUND AND LIGHT SHOW begins after dusk. Sitting in a small amphitheatre, you watch colored lights dramatically illuminate the pyramids, Sphinx, and ruined temples while a recorded sound system tells their story with a musical accompaniment. The narration is given in English, French, German, and Arabic on different nights of the week. But even if it's not the night for your language, the music and the lights and the monuments set a mood which helps your imagination bridge the centuries. Unfortunately, the mood is broken by photographic idiots vainly attempting to illuminate the entire scene with flashcubes so they can record it on their Instamatics. It's ironic that photography is banned in so many places where it doesn't matter, yet is allowed here where it spoils the effect.

What is a vacation without shopping? In Cairo the place to do it is the KHAN EL KHALILI BAZAAR. Hundreds of shops in this maze of narrow streets sell everything you could want, and lots of things you didn't know you wanted. At first glance the bazaar might be disappointing because it doesn't look old enough. I expected something like the Cairo depicted in "Raiders of the Lost Ark," but discovered later that the movie's bazaar scene was filmed in Tunisia.

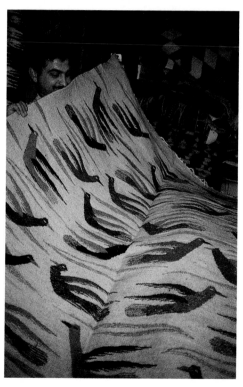

Local crafts make excellent gifts and souvenirs of Egypt. They include jewelry, brassware, leather, alabaster, cotton goods, carpets, and papyrus paintings. Don't expect to find any genuine Egyptian antiquities; trade in them is strictly forbidden. But many excellent reproductions are on sale. One of the most popular gifts for a lady is a gold pendant in the form of a cartouche, with her name inscribed in hieoroglyphics.

Half the fun of shopping in the bazaar is bargaining (see sidebar). The asking price is only a starting point, and it's easy to do comparison shop-

Among the local crafts for sale are carpets, brasswork, and jewelry.

BARGAINING

If you pay an Egyptian merchant the price he asks, he will probably be disappointed. Half the fun of buying and selling at the bazaar is bargaining. It is a traditional and expected part of commerce in the Middle East, especially where tourists are involved. Initial prices are almost always inflated, sometimes up to 1,000 percent by the hawkers at Luxor or the Pyramids. Street vendors are sometimes persistent to the point of being obnoxious. They may not take "Imshee" ("Go away!") for an answer. One technique that can be effective is to point a camera at them. Many are unlicensed and don't want their picture taken.

At the bazaars, all bargaining is done in a good-natured way. Merchants aren't insulted when you offer less than they ask, and if they lose a sale, malesh. Start by offering considerably less than the asking price, then wheel and deal from there, but don't show that you really want an item. If all else fails, walk out. The merchant may make an offer you can't refuse.

Some stores advertise "fixed prices", but even they are sometimes open to bargaining. It won't hurt to try.

Bargaining is also effective with cab drivers. They always charge tourists more than locals, but if you know the going rate you will get a better deal. However, the deal is never over till the money changes hands. Drivers will often play on your guilt feelings, attempting to get a bigger tip.

ping. Stores selling a certain item, perfumes for example, are usually located on the same street; so it is easy to go back and forth to check quality and prices. Don't get the impression that Khan el Khalili is a tourist trap; Egyptians also come here to shop.

Your tour guide or taxi driver will probably recommend a certain store where you can get a good deal (and he can get a kickback). Actually, he will receive a kickback from any store in which you buy something as long as he accompanies you inside. Don't be concerned; that's just the local way of doing business. Consider it a part of his tip.

The tomb of Anwar Sadat is located across the street from the reviewing stand where he was assasinated in 1981.

Although they are proud of their ancient heritage, today's Egyptians identify more with their Islamic traditions than those of the Pharaohs. In order to understand and appreciate this, you should visit some historic mosques. Most tours of Islamic Cairo begin at THE CITADEL. A fortress built by Saladin during the 12th century on a hill overlooking the city, the walls are said to be made of stones taken from the Pyramids. The top of the wall affords a panoramic view of Cairo; you can often see the Pyramids off in the distance through the haze. Inside the fortress are museums, military installations, and palaces of former rulers.

The dominant building is the MUHAMMED ALI MOSQUE. Patterned after the historic Istanbul mosque, it was built in the 19th century by one of Egypt's most influential rulers (no relation to the former heavyweight champion). The original Muhammed Ali is buried in a corner of the mosque. Although students of Islamic architecture disparage the mosque as too gaudy and too recent, I was awed when looking up at the high, ornate dome. Standing inside the cavernous structure, even a nonbeliever has to be impressed by the faith that built such an imposing monument.

215

The Mohammed Ali Mosque is the centerpiece of The Citadel, a fortress built by Saladin to repel the crusaders.

The IBN TULUN MOSQUE represents Islamic architecture at its finest. Located near the Citadel's western gate, this structure was originally built in 879 AD. Restorations have been faithful to the original; it is considered Cairo's oldest mosque as well as its most beautiful. The simple open courtyard has a central fountain, and is surrounded by an arcade with carved stucco arches. Walk through the arcade and view the courtyard through the frame of the arches. A minaret is located on the northwest wall, and some baksheesh will allow you to climb the outside spiral staircase for a breathtaking view. If you see only one mosque in Cairo, make it Ibn Tulun.

Cairo is a night city, especially in summer. Cool breezes make it a pleasant time to go out walking, eating, or just meeting friends. The local people eat late and play later. One of the best ways to enjoy the time is an EVENING CRUISE ON A FELUCCA. Feluccas are the Nile sailing boats which have changed little since ancient times. The river's current runs north, the prevailing winds blow toward the south. Therefore the boats always sail upstream, and drift with the current when going

216

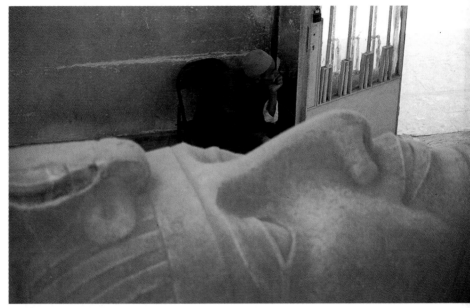

At Memphis, the former capitol of Egypt, a giant statue of Ramses II lies in repose.

down. One of our most memorable evenings was such a ride, arranged by a diving friend who lives in Cairo. He hired the boat and brought along a delicious picnic dinner of local specialties including lamb, eggplant dishes, salads, and baclava for dessert. Watching the lights of Cairo go by from the peaceful calm of the river lends an entirely different perspective to this city of many faces. Just remember to bring insect repellent, because the mosquitoes love the river too.

If you have an extra day, visit SAKKARA, about an hour's drive south of Cairo. This vast archaeological site includes the Step Pyramid of Zoser. The first of the pyramids, it is the oldest existing stone structure in the world, dating back almost 5,000 years. The site also includes a striking temple designed by the great architect, Imhotep, who was later worshipped as a deity. There are also tombs with wall carvings and paintings. If you can't make it to Luxor, this will be your only chance to visit ancient tombs. On the way back, stop at KERDASSA, a small village of craftsmen and artisans, and watch rugs being woven. Prices may be lower than Khan el Khalili.

EFFICIENCY IN CAIRO

Cairo overwhelms the first-time tourist. The noise, dust, congestion and traffic intimidate him. He hesitates to leave the air-conditioned cocoon of the Sheraton or Hilton. The overriding impression is that nothing in the city works, and that the residents lead a miserable existence. But like any big city, residents have found ways to cope. With all its faults, they are proud of the city and of their ability to make it work. In some ways, Cairo works better than New York, London, or Frankfurt.

We were at Cairo airport to meet Mia, who was arriving from the United States at 2 PM. When we got there we discovered the flight would be an hour late. Malesh. My friend, Ali Saad El Din, announced that this would give him time to have a new exhaust system installed on his aging Fiat. "The heat has gotten to you," I declared. "There's no way you'll get to a mechanic and back within an hour, much less find an exhaust system for this old clunker which has been out of production for ten years."

Ali chided me for my lack of faith and assured that we would be back in time to meet Mia's flight, even if he had to return without an exhaust system. Reluctantly I climbed into the vintage Fiat and we took off with a roar that sounded like a B 17 bomber. Ali drove to the back streets of Heliopolis, where a four-block area of tiny storefronts housed nothing but small mechanics' shops. Some did body work, some did radiators, some did exhaust systems. Nearly all the work was being done in the street. It was just like a huge bazaar, except everything revolved around automobiles.

We stopped at an exhaust specialist's shop where Ali negotiated, didn't like the price, and drove on to another one. At the second place he made a deal. "I told him," he explained, "if he doesn't have it finished in 20 minutes, I'd drive off without paying him." The mechanic cut off the Fiat's exhaust system with a torch. He then went into his shop and came out with a straight pipe of the same diameter, and a small homemade muffler. Laying the pipe on the sidewalk next to the Fiat's, he bent a little here and cut a little there until it matched.

The descriptions above just scratch the surface of things to do in Cairo. It will take three days just to see the sights discussed here. If you have more time, purchase a general guidebook; then go out and discover more about one of the most fascinating cities on earth.

LUXOR

Because the Nile flows north, the southern part of the country is called Upper Egypt. A trip there is one in time as well as space. People live more simply. Most of them work the land essentially the way their ancestors did hundreds of years ago. Men wear the traditional galabiyahs instead of western clothes; married women wear black and cover their heads. Donkeys and carts are the favored means of transportation.

Egypt Air offers daily flights from Cairo to Luxor, or you can ride an air-conditioned overnight sleeper train. You probably won't find a taxi when your train arrives. Instead, the ride to your hotel will be in a horse-drawn carriage called a hantour. The contrast of the modern, air-conditioned sleeper train to a dirt plaza and a horse-drawn carriage will prepare you for the sights of Upper Egypt.

A Nile cruise ship docks at Luxor. Across the Nile, on the west bank, is the Valley of the Kings.

Luxor was the capital of ancient Egypt for a long period of its history. (Memphis and Tel El Armana also served as capitals.) On the east bank are two magnificent temples: the Temple of Luxor and the Temple of Amun Ra at Karnak, along with a fine museum. On the west bank are the Valleys of the Kings, Queens, and Nobles, along with the Colossi of Memnon, and the funerary temples of Hatshepsut, Seti I, and Ramses III, and the Temple of Medinet Habu. There is much to see and do.

One of the most pleasant ways to experience Upper Egypt is on a Nile Cruiser. Over 80 ships ply the waters on a regular schedule, ranging from small paddlewheelers to huge floating hotels. The biggest and most luxurious ships are air conditioned, have four decks of staterooms, a bar, a restaurant, and even a swimming pool on the sundeck. Meals are sumptuous buffets; you will gain a few pounds unless your willpower is up to the challenge. Prices for the four-day cruise between Luxor and Aswan include all meals and sightseeing— everything except liquor. The ships stop at the temples of Esna, Edfu, and Kom Ombo along the way. Tour guides are extremely knowledgeable, speaking fluent English, German or French, depending on the nationality of the tourists. All have a college degree in archaeology, but make more money this way than by doing research.

Comfortably settled in your beach chair on the sundeck, a panorama of life along the Nile unfolds before you. Fellahin (farmers) work their fields with primitive plows pulled by oxen. Cattle-driven Archimedes screws lift water up to the fields from irrigation channels. Fishermen beat the water with sticks to drive fish into their nets. In the evening, women and girls come down to the riverbank, carrying earthen pots on their heads to fetch water. All life seems to be centered around the river. Ancient Egypt lives on, not only in its stone ruins but also in the lives of the fellahin. You feel as though you were in a time warp, going back 100, 1,000, even 3,000 years.

THE HAGG

Every devout Muslim plans to make a pilgrimage to Mecca at least once in his lifetime. The pilgrimage is called the Hagg, one who has made it is a Hajj. The Hajj is cleansed of past sins and is prepared to live the rest of his life in purity. To demonstrate his status to the community, he often paints his home with scenes from the journey.

The practice is more prevalent in the villages than in Cairo. Some of the designs are quite ornate and really stand out from the surrounding houses. In Gurna, where it never rains, houses are made of sun-dried mud bricks. Most of them are the same dull brown as the surrounding sand. But the houses of the Hajj are whitewashed, and on the walls are beautiful paintings depicting the trip. They show the means of transportation, either an airplane or a ship. Many show the Kaabah, the holy shrine in Mecca. Paintings might also display other aspects of the trip. One hajj went on an African safari before or after the journey, so his home is decorated with pictures of lions and giraffes. Others paint religious symbols or something about their work. Look for them in Luxor or in the small towns around Cairo. The painted homes display an important aspect of Egypt's spiritual life.

In Upper Egypt villages, many houses are decorated with scenes from the owner's pilgrimage to Mecca. This one is in Quesir on the Red Sea.

To fully describe the anitiquities of Luxor would easily take an entire book this size. An excellent one is available, entitled *Luxor: A Guide to Ancient Thebes* by Jill Kamil. The author describes all the major temples and tombs in exquisite detail. Published in England, the book is sold in Cairo and Luxor bookstores. Michael von Haag's *Travelaid Guide to Egypt* also contains fine descriptions and history, and includes interesting personal vignettes. Both paperbacks are wonderful companions on a trip to Luxor. Leaving the details to the experts, I will only touch on some highlights.

If you have only two days in Luxor, spend one on the east bank and the other on the west. Begin with a tour of Karnak, Egypt's largest and grandest temple, which took over 250 years to build. Visit Luxor Temple in late afternoon when the warm light and long shadows cast their spell on the ancient columns. The small, modern museum in town is a direct contrast to the one in Cairo, with a limited number of displays beautifully presented and lit.

222

At night, don't miss the Sound and Light Show at Karnak. Far better than the one at the Pyramids, you will walk through the temple, stopping at various stations to watch the colored lights bring the stones to life as disembodied voices and music retell old legends. At the final station, you sit on benches overlooking the sacred lake that reflects the vast panorama before you. Even if you don't catch the English version, the eloquent pillars, statues, walls, and obelisks tell their own story. If only the flashcube morons would stay home...

In ancient Egyptian mythology, the east bank of the Nile — where the rising sun symbolizes rebirth — was for the living; the west bank for the

The magnificent temple of Karnak took over 250 years, and 13 different pharaohs, to complete construction. It is the largest of Egypt's surviving temples.

dead. All the tombs and pyramids are located on the side of the setting sun. Across the river from Luxor, the kings, queens and nobles of the empire were buried in tombs carved into the mountainsides. The pyramid building era lasted only 200 years, when Memphis (near today's Cairo) was the capitol. Later pharaohs had tunnels dug into solid rock, decorated by craftsmen and artisans, then buried and hidden. None of them completely escaped the ravages of the robbers; only that of Tutankhamen came close. An insignificant boy king, Tutankhamen died at the age of 18, but the treasures buried with him proved one of the great archaeological finds of all time. His tomb is one of the smallest in the Valley of the Kings. Just imagine the riches that must have been buried with some of the great pharaohs like Seti I, whose tomb is ten times the size of Tutankhamen's.

223

Tour groups generally overrun the west bank in the morning. Each tomb will have about 50 people inside with another 50 waiting to get in. That is hardly conducive to studying the intricate paintings and reliefs which cover the walls. Although they were done over 3,000 years ago and have not been restored, some of the pigments are so vivid they look as though the paint is scarcely dry. Some are unfinished because a body had to be buried within 70 days of death. It is fascinating to see the rough sketches and the grids drawn in red, which were used to enlarge the paintings from preliminary drawings.

In order to get a better look, Mia and I returned to the valley one afternoon. We rode the Peoples' Ferry across the river for a few piastres; then bargained with a cab driver to take us to the various sites. One can also rent bicycles or donkeys instead of cabs. Although more adventurous, they aren't feasible in sum-

The tomb of Seti I is about ten times the size of Tutankhamen's. Imagine what treasures it must have held.

When photography was allowed in the tombs, an accomodating guard held a reflector.

mer when the west bank becomes an oven. The old saw about mad dogs and Englishmen could have been invented in the Valley of the Kings; the temperature on a summer afternoon is usually over 110 degrees. There were only three other tourists in the entire valley. We had the tombs completely to ourselves, and were able to view the paintings in detail while reading about them in the guidebook. In a couple of tombs the lights weren't on but the gates were unlocked, so we entered with flashlights. It took me back to the Saturday matinees of my childhood, sitting terrified in a theater while The Mummy stalked the silver screen. Moving further into the tunnels, we could imagine how Howard Carter must have felt when entering Tutankhamen's tomb for the first time.

The guards even allowed us to enter a tomb usually closed to tourists, that of Thutmose III. Located over a ravine between two steep cliffs, a high iron staircase leads to the entrance. The guard unlocked the rusty gate, turned on the lights, and waited outside while we entered the narrow tunnel. Looking at the wall paintings, we imagined what would happen if we were locked in. How long before the next person would come in to find our bodies? Imagination sometimes gets the better of you inside the tombs because when we finished, the guard was waiting for us with a smile. He was probably surprised by the generous baksheesh he received.

If you make an afternoon visit to the west bank in summer, bring at least a quart and a half of water per person and move slowly. Protect yourself from the intense sun with a hat and sunglasses. It is considerably cooler in the tombs, so use the time inside to rest and cool off. Winter is the high season for tourism in Upper Egypt, so the valley will probably be just as crowded in the afternoon as in the morning.

On our early trips, cameras were allowed inside all the tombs except Tut's (because his mummy lies inside). Flash was forbidden because of its possible effect on the pigments. Instead, a mirror was placed at the entrance. A guard held a piece of cardboard covered with aluminum foil, which reflected the sun's rays on the paintings for photography. (Of course, some baksheesh

The Collosi of Memnon guard the entrance to the Valley of the Kings. They are all that is left of a great temple.

was expected.) A minute of reflected sunlight probably fades the pigments far more than a thousandth of a second of strobe light, but those were the rules at the time. A year later, all photography inside the tombs was forbidden. If that's what it takes to preserve these priceless works of art, no one should complain. Rules are subject to change, so check the current status. Remember, however, that slides of the tombs' interiors are available at gift shops throughout Egypt.

The Valleys of the Queens and the Nobles also lie on the west bank. The Valley of the Nobles is the more interesting because its tomb paintings depict daily life in ancient Egypt. They show the people farming, hunting, dancing, feasting, and doing all the things common people do. One can identify with them more readily than with the kings and queens preparing to meet their gods.

The village of Gurna was built right over the tombs of the nobles. For generations, families there were said to have systematically plundered the tombs and sold their treasures to antiquities dealers. The novel, *Sphinx*, by Robin Cook, is based on that premise. During our first visit there, we met a cute little seven-year-old girl who tried to give Mia her homemade doll, then asked fifty piastres for it. We felt guilty and refused the offer, but took her picture. A year later we met the same girl, now eight years old with more street sense. She had learned some English from tourists and now demanded baksheesh to have her picture taken. I refused on general principles, and she immediately began to cry. Thoroughly flustered, I gave her all my change. She probably laughed all the way to the piggy bank.

PHOTOGRAPHING PEOPLE

People pictures are often among the most memorable brought back from a vacation. In Egypt it isn't easy. Most Egyptians don't like to be photographed by tourists. Some of them will pose only for baksheesh. The main objection seems to be that they are self-conscious about their poverty. Too many western magazines have spotlighted that aspect of modern Egypt in photographic essays. They object to being depicted as poor, backward people. Rural women are especially camera shy.

Fortunately, children and old men usually don't have that problem. They often make the best subjects anyway. I usually ask permission to take someone's photograph before shooting. If they refuse, I honor their wishes.

Many people are interested in receiving a copy of their picture. A good way to accommodate them is to bring along a Polaroid camera and give them instant prints. It's a great icebreaker.

Town markets are an excellent place for photographs. In some of the small villages, away from tourist attractions, no one is camera shy. People seem happy that you care enough about them to take a picture. But as tourism continues to grow, these places may become exceedingly rare.

Often it seems that the more imposing your camera equipment, the more people resent it. They seem to feel less threatened by simple cameras. On my last trip I brought a small automated camera 35mm that could be operated with one hand. It looks like a toy, but takes excellent pictures when used within its limitations. It allowed me to shoot street scenes that would have been impossible with an SLR.

Along the banks of the Nile, a cattle driven water wheel provides irrigation.

Don't miss the Temple of Hatshepsut, Egypt's only female pharaoh. The majestic edifice is dramatically located at the foot of a sheer cliff at Deir el Bahri. She sent an expedition on the Red Sea to the land of Punt. An entire wall of the temple is devoted to carvings depicting that expedition. They show her troops on sailing craft, with tropical fish swimming in the waters below them. You will be able to recognize most of them. The final frieze in the series shows the queen of Punt being brought before Hatshepsut. Her legs are grossly swollen, probably the result of elephantiasis.

Many kids go through a stage when they want to become an archaeologist. Luxor allows us to relive these childhood fantasies. It is impossible to leave without increased interest and knowledge about ancient Egypt.

ASWAN

Aswan is the southernmost major city in Egypt. Its most important landmark is the High Dam, built to control the Nile flood and generate electricity for much of the country. Behind it, the dammed river forms 300- mile-long Lake Nasser. Two major temples, threatened with flooding by the dam, were moved to higher ground by international cooperative ventures. The most famous is Abu Simbel, 172 miles south of Aswan. The trip takes about a half hour on an Egypt Air jet. You are herded into buses for the ride to the ticket booths, where you pay admission, including a special Abu Simbel Town Council Tax. The guides run you through a quickie tour of the two temples: The Temple of Abu Simbel and the Temple of Hathor. Our guide seemed detached and bored, speaking like a 33 RPM record on 45. Within two hours you are back on the plane headed for Aswan. Is it worth it? Yes.

Carved out of solid rock by Ramses II, the temple would have been flooded by the rising waters of Lake Nasser. An international salvage team completely dismantled and reconstructed it on higher ground, setting it into the side of a hollow mountain built to recreate the original landscape. The project — coordinated by UNESCO — was completed in 1967 at a cost of 42 million dollars. Standing at the foot of the four massive Ramses statues, it is impossible to tell where the rocks were cut apart and rejoined. Even the graffiti of ancient Greeks and 19th century Europeans is intact. The temple was reconstucted with the same orientation to the sun as the original site. On February 22 and October 22 each year, the first rays of the rising sun penetrate 100 meters to the inner sanctum and illuminate statues of the four gods inside.

Also saved from flooding was the Temple of Philae, now located on an island between the High Dam and the British Dam, which was built at the turn of the century. The temple, constructed during Ptolemaic times, was dedicated to the Goddess Hathor. One of the most beautiful temples in Egypt, it was also dismantled and moved to higher ground through a UNESCO project. Financing came from the proceeds of the Tutankhamen exhibition that toured the United States from 1976 to 1979.

The granite islands in the Aswan area make for a pleasant felucca ride. One interesting stop is Kitchener's Island with its botanical gardens of tropical plants. An anomaly in the desert environment, the gardens were the pet project of Britain's consul-general at the turn of the century, Lord Kitchener. Botany was his lifelong passion, and he indulged it on the island where he lived. The gardens attract flocks of exotic birds, including snowy egrets which literally fill some of the trees.

Other sites to visit near Aswan include the High Dam, the exquisite Aga Khan Mausoleum, and the Nubian Villages. Many Nubians, the black citizens of Egypt, were displaced by the dam as the waters of Lake Nasser flooded their homeland. The government built villages for them near Aswan and many of them work in the city. But one village chief remarked, "We were better off before, because then we had land to grow crops on."

Aswan is a renowned winter resort for Europeans and Asians. In the summer it is one of the hottest places in Egypt. The mean high temperature in August is 106 degrees. The main reasons to go at that time would be to visit Abu Simbel or to begin or end a Nile cruise.

ALONG THE WAY

If time permits, visit the temples of Edfu, Esna and Kom Ombo, located between Luxor and Aswan. They are included on the Nile cruise, but if you are going by car and have the opportunity, stop there. All were built during the time of the Greek pharaohs, the Ptolemeys. The Temple of Khnum is in a pit in the center of the town of Esna, with local residences above it. Like many of the ancient temples, Esna was later used as a place of worship by the Copts, an early Christian sect. They defaced the carvings of the ancient gods wherever they could reach them and carved their own crosses into the walls. Only the carvings that were buried in the sand and those too high to reach were spared.

The Temple of Horus at Edfu is the most intact in all of Egypt. Built by the Greeks in an attempt to re-create the style of the earlier Egyptians, it is degraded by archaeological purists but was extremely impressive to my untrained eye. This site is located halfway between Luxor and Aswan. The third temple, Kom Ombo, celebrates a crocodile god.

By taxi, the trip from Luxor to Hurghada takes three and a

Most Nubians live in Upper Egypt, near Aswan. Many of their tribal lands now lie under the waters of Lake Nasser.

half hours If time permits, make a small detour and visit the Temple of Hathor at Dendera. Rising out of a sea of sugar cane fields, this gem is off the beaten tourist path. The temple spans the New Kingdom, the Ptolemeys, and the Copts. Nearly as well preserved as Edfu, there are secret stairs and passageways, which the guard will show you on a slow day for a little baksheesh. Some of the best carvings, with original pigment remaining, are in a chamber below the temple. Carvings above the level the Copts could reach are intact, but the prudish early Christians hacked the genitals off most of them. The ceiling of some chambers were home for hundreds of bats.

Outside the Dendera temple is a Nilometer, a tunnel with stairs leading down to the water table. Ancient rulers used it to measure the level of the river, and taxed the people accordingly. Since the pharaohs were kin to the Gods, they took credit for the annual floods and demanded a share of the wealth in good years. A sacred lake is also on the site. Filled by the Nile flood, it must have been a primitive swimming pool with rock walls. It is perfectly rectangular; the ancients could have held swim meets there if they were so inclined. Today, with the controlled water table, it is filled with palm trees like a small oasis.

On the road from Dendera to Hurghada, our taxi driver gave us his succinct view of Egyptian-American relations. Pointing to the Koran on his dash, he said, "We have a book, you have a book. The Russians have no book. We are cousins."

APPENDIX A

GLOSSARY OF ARABIC TERMS

Most guidebooks to Egypt include a glossary of basic Arabic that the traveler can utilize for basic survival needs. They include such phrases as "Please," "Hello," and "Where is the toilet?" The reader is referred to those books for those phrases. Most dive guides speak excellent English. However many dive sites have Arabic names, and an understanding of them can enhance a diver's appreciation. Some crew members of the dive boats speak only Arabic, and it may be necessary to communicate with them regarding equipment or logistical support. For those reasons, the following glossary is presented.

A word about spelling is in order. Arabic has some sounds which have no equivalent in English. Therefore, it is impossible to exactly transliterate Arabic into English letters; the same word will be spelled several different ways. In this glossary, I have attempted to spell the words as closely as possible to the way they are pronounced.

GEOGRAPHICAL TERMS

El Bahr el Akhmar: The Red Sea
Dishet: Hill or mountain
Erg: Reef or shoal
Fandera: A large rock, or a small islet
Gebel, Jebel: Mountain
Ghezirat: Island
Ghubbet, Khalij: Bay
Kad: Shoal or spit of land
Kahf: Large cave
Madiq: Strait
Marsa: Harbor or anchorage
Qa: Bottom
Qad: Shoal
Ras: Point, cape, peak, headland
Sha'ab: Reef, rocky shoal
Sharm: Inlet, bay
Wadi: Valley or river course

WIND AND WEATHER

Azyab or Khamseen: A hot, dry wind off the desert, causing rough seas.
Bard: Cold
Dafee: Warm
Hahr: Hot
Moog or Amwag: Waves
Smoom: Same as azyab. Literally, smoom means poison
Shamal: The prevailing winds from the north
Tiyahr: Current

DIVING TERMS:

Adehd: Gauge
Ami'k: Deep
Anbubah rhats: Scuba tank
Anbubah malee'ah: full tank
Anbubah farehra: empty tank
Bedla rhats: Wet suit (literally, diving suit)
Dakh'l: Shallow:
Dakht el Maya: Underwater
Emle: Fill
Ghersh: Shark
Ha'it or Ghadahr: Wall
Howah: Air
Kamera: Camera
Makina dokht howah: Compressor (literally, machine
                           to compress air)
Markib: Ship
Markib Rheraan: Shipwreck
Maya: Water
Nadara: Mask (literally, glasses)
Omkh: Depth
Rhats: Diving
Rhoeah: Visibility
Sat'h: Surface
Samak: Fish
Zhanif: Fin
Zorah: Boat

APPENDIX B

A RED SEA BIBLIOGRAPHY

The better prepared you are for a trip, the more you will enjoy it. One of the best ways is to learn about the things you are about to see and experience through books. Following is a selection of books which will be helpful in gathering information about Egypt and the Red Sea.

EGYPTIAN HISTORY

Jules D. Billard, Editor: *Ancient Egypt* Washington, DC: National Geographic Society, 1978. A lush, beautiful coffee table book with text to match its pictures, this volume presents Egyptian archaeology in a concise, understandable manner for the layman.

Howard Carter, *The Tomb of Tutankhamen* New York: E.P. Dutton, 1972. A reprint of a book completed in 1933, this tells of the discovery of Tutankhamen's tomb by the man who did it.

Alan Moorehead, *The Blue Nile* New York: Harper & Row, 1962 The history of Egypt from 1798 to 1856 tells of the violence, high adventure, and interesting characters of the 19th century.

John Romer, *Valley of the Kings* New York: William Morrow Company, 1981. An archaeologist tells the history of archaeology in the Valley of the Kings.

Mohammed Saleh and Hourig Sourouzian, *Official Catalog of the Egyptian Museum, Cairo* Mainz: Verlag Philipp von Zabern, 1987. A wonderful souvenir of your museum trip, this book spotlights 270 of the most significant exhibits in words and photographs.

EGYPT (GENERAL)

Fred Maroon and P. H. Newby, *The Egypt Story* New York: Chanticleer Press, 1981 A coffee-table book on modern Egypt, including a look at ancient monuments, the exquisite photographs are all done with natural light.

RED SEA

Gunnar Bemert and Rupert Ormond, *Red Sea Coral Reefs*, London: Kegan Paul International, 1981. This is the only book of its kind, with color pictures and text covering the creatures of the Red Sea reefs and their behavior, as observed along the coast of Saudi Arabia.

Shlomo Cohen, *Red Sea Divers' Guide* Tel Aviv: Seapen Books, 1988 revised edition. A do-it-yourself guide, the color maps and photos cover beach diving in the Gulf of Aquaba.

Helmut Debelius: *Underwater Guide to Red Sea Fishes* Stuttgart: Verlag Stephanie Naglshmid, 1987. A pocket-sized guidebook to Red Sea fishes, beautifully illustrated with color photographs. Although not as comprehensive as Randall's, all photos of fish in this volume were shot underwater, in their natural environment.

Alistair J. Edwards & Stephen M. Head, editors: *The Red Sea* Oxford: Pergamon Press, 1987. A collection of overview articles on subjects ranging from geology and oceanography to invertebrates, fishes, and human settlement. Primarily intended for scientists, a serious student will find this the best source of in-depth information on this area.

David Pilisoff, *Samantha* Tel Aviv: Lorenz and Pilisoff, 1977. An Israeli photographer shot and wrote this book on one of the Red Sea's most beautiful creatures, an Australian model tastefully posing in the buff.

Dr. John Randall, *Red Sea Reef Fishes* London: Immel Publishing, 1983. One of the world's leading icthyologists, Randall photographs and identifies most of the common fishes of the Red Sea.

Dr. Peter Vine, *Red Sea Invertebrates* London: Immel Publishing, 1986. Vine does the same with invertebrates as Randall did with fishes in this beautifully illustrated book.

RED SEA DIVING HISTORY

Dr. Eugenie Clark, *Lady with a Spear* New York: Harper & Bros, 1953. The pioneer diving scientist tells about her experiences in Hurghada in the early 1950s.

Jacques Cousteau, *The Silent World* New York: Harper & Bros. 1953. Some of Cousteau's early voyages were to the Red Sea and are covered in this classic book.

Jacques Cousteau and James Dugan, *The Living Sea* New York: Harper & Row, 1963. Cousteau recalls early trips to the Egyptian Red Sea, including The Brothers and Daedalus Reef.

Hans Hass, *Manta: Under the Red Sea with Spear and Camera* Chicago: Rand McNally, 1953, Hass tells of his first Red Sea expedition, diving with a rebreather from Port Sudan.

GUIDEBOOKS

Recommended guidebooks are described in Chapter II of the text.